The
Practical
Stylist

Also by Sheridan Baker

The Complete Stylist, SECOND EDITION

The Essayist, SECOND EDITION

Problems in Exposition: Supplementary Exercises for The Complete Stylist *and* The Practical Stylist
(WITH DWIGHT STEVENSON)

The Practical Stylist

Third Edition

SHERIDAN BAKER
The University of Michigan

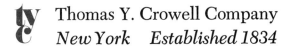
Thomas Y. Crowell Company
New York   Established 1834

Library of Congress Cataloging in Publication Data

Baker, Sheridan Warner
  The practical stylist.

  1. English language—Rhetoric.   I. Title.
PE1408.B285   1973   808'.042   72–10863
ISBN 0–690–65002–7
ISBN 0–690–65001–9 (paper)

To Sally

DESIGNED BY ANGELA FOOTE

Manufactured in the United States of America

2   3   4   5   6   7   8   9   10

Preface

This is a rhetoric primarily for freshman English, but it has also proved useful to the advanced student, to people in business and government, and to many others who have found themselves facing a blank page and the problems of exposition. From the freshman's first essay through the senior's last paper (and on through the doctoral dissertation and the corporate annual report), the expository problems are always the same. Indeed, they all come down to two fundamental questions: one of form, one of style. And even form is spatial styling. Since, in general, writing well is writing in style, I have found it practical to teach writing almost as a tactile act, in which the student learns how to shape his material and bring out the grain to best advantage. Hence *The Practical Stylist*—again revised extensively.

To the Third Edition I have added a number of exercises throughout, and a new brief chapter, "Evidence," to expand an issue essential to the first three chapters, at a point where a number of teachers and students have asked for further consolidation. To Chapter 9, "The Research Paper," I have added a complete sample research paper, which should provide a stronger focus for the discussion of research mechanics. I have transferred sections on grammar and spelling to the appendices, to improve the flow of ideas from chapter to chapter, and I have brought "A Glossary of Usage" up to date. Because they seem difficult to teach effectively, I have dropped a few things here and there, such as "Three Excursions" (the "terrible essay" is retained as an exercise at the end of Chapter 8). But in its content, its size, and its practical intent, *The Practical Stylist* remains essentially the same.

I mean the book to be practical also in its brevity. Most handbooks on writing seem too big, too wordy, too involved. They seem to get mired in their own diligence and to stay stuck on the student's shelf. This book aims to travel light, to cover the ground without inordinate deliberation. I have included only what seems useful and essential.

To be sure, I omit some of the pedagogical favorites, such as definition and syllogistic reasoning, because I believe them secondary to more basic processes, which in fact manage most of the refinements without worrying about them. I emphasize argument, because I believe that argument subsumes all other expository principles and that it teaches clearly and easily the firmest organization. So I begin with the argumentative thesis and include only a few exercises in simple exposition.

Many handbooks begin with simple units and build upward. I have found the opposite approach far more efficient. Once the student can push his material into a single argumentative thesis and can grasp the large essentials of structural arrangement, he then can proceed easily to the smaller and smaller elements, which get the more powerful as they decrease in size—to paragraphs, to sentences and their punctuation, and on to the heart of the matter, to words, where the real dynamite of rhetoric is.

I have included exercises in thesis-making, in paragraphing, in writing various kinds of sentences and punctuating them, in using words and spelling them, in handling various figures of speech. I have tried to encourage the student to play with language, to write unusual and complicated sentences for exercise, to juggle with words, much as the new courses in elementary mathematics start with numerical games and puzzles. The chapter on the research paper then draws these points together, bringing the student's expository skills fully to bear. The book concludes with the three appendices—on grammar, spelling and capitalization, and usage—for supplement and permanent reference, with further exercises as needed. Inside the front cover is a list against which the student may check his work; inside the back cover, a set of symbols for marking errors. The book serves well alone, especially if the teacher likes to concentrate on his students' writing in weekly essays arising from the exercises, or in company with readings in literature.

The teacher will find plenty of room for his own course. He will undoubtedly find opportunity for that almost necessary bonus of academic gratification, disagreeing with the book, out of which much of our best teaching comes. He will certainly find a great deal that is familiar. Nothing here is really new; I am simply describing the natural linguistic facts discovered again and again by the heirs of Aristotle, in which lineage I seem inescapably to belong. For I have found that the one practical need in all writing is to mediate gracefully between opposite possibilities—between simplicity and complexity, clarity and shade, economy and plenitude, the particular and the general. I hope this book will help student and teacher to shoot the wickets pleasantly and well.

I wish to acknowledge my great debt to the teachers who, from the testing of some twenty-five thousand classrooms, have given me their encouragement and their suggestions. I am no less grateful to the many individual students and private citizens who have written me from as far away as Kenya and as near home as Ann Arbor.

SHERIDAN BAKER

Contents

1
Thesis

The Stylistic Approach

Style in writing is something like style in a car, a woman, or a Greek temple—the ordinary materials of this world so poised and perfected as to stand out from the landscape and compel a second look, something that hangs in the reader's mind, like a vision. It is an idea made visible, and polished to its natural beauty. It is your own voice, with the hems and haws chipped out, speaking the common language uncommonly well. It takes a craftsman who has discovered the knots and potentials in his material, one who has learned to like words as some people like polished wood or stones, one who has learned to enjoy phrasing and syntax, and the very punctuation that keeps them straight. It is a labor of love, and like love it can bring pleasure and satisfaction. Once you have learned to enjoy the work, you will please others. You will convince and delight, and get more than one admiring look.

Style is not for the gifted only. Quite the contrary. Writing indeed has a certain mystery about it, just as life does. But the stylistic side of writing is, in fact, the only side that can be analyzed and learned. The stylistic approach is the practical approach: you learn some things to do and not to do, as you would learn strokes in tennis. Your ultimate game is up to you, but you can at least begin in good form. Naturally, it takes practice. You have to keep at it. Like the doctor and the lawyer and the golfer and the tennis player, you just keep practicing—even to write a practically perfect letter. But if you like the game, you can probably learn to play it well. You will at least be able to write a respectable sentence, and to express your thoughts clearly, without puffing and flailing.

In the essay, as in business, trying to get started and getting off on the wrong foot account for most of our lost motion. So you will start by learning how to find a thesis, which will virtually organize your essay for you. Next you will study the relatively simple structure of the essay, and the structure of the paragraph—the architecture of spatial styling. Then, for exercise, you will experiment with various styles of sentence, playing with length and complexity. And finally you will get down to words themselves. Here is where writing tells; and here, as in ancient times, you will be in touch with the mystery. But again, there are things to do and things not to do, and these can be learned. So, to begin.

Where Essays Fail

You can usually blame a bad essay on a bad beginning. If your essay falls apart, it probably has no primary idea to hold it together. "What's the big idea?" we used to ask. The phrase will serve as a reminder that you must find the "big idea" behind your several smaller thoughts and musings before you start to write. In the beginning was the *logos*, says the Bible—the idea, the plan, caught in a flash as if in a single word. Find your *logos*, and you are ready to round out your essay and set it spinning.

The central idea, or thesis, is your essay's life and spirit. If your thesis is sufficiently clear, it will organize your material almost automatically and so obviate elaborate planning. If you do not find a thesis, your essay will be a tour through the miscellaneous. An essay replete with scaffolds and catwalks—"We have just seen this; now let us turn to this"—is an essay in which the inhering idea is weak or nonexistent. A purely expository and descriptive essay, one simply about "Cats," for instance, will have to rely on outer scaffolding alone (some orderly progression from Persia to Siam), since it really has no idea at all. It is all subject, all cats, instead of an embodied idea *about* cats.

The Argumentative Edge

Find your thesis.

The *about*-ness puts an argumentative edge on the subject. When you have something to say *about* cats, you have found your underlying idea. You have something to defend, something to fight about: not just "Cats," but "The cat is really man's best friend." Now the hackles on all dog men are rising, and you have an argument on your hands. You have something to prove. You have a thesis.

"What's the big idea, Mac?" Let the impudence in that time-honored demand remind you that the best thesis is a kind of affront to somebody. No one will be very much interested in listening to you deplete the thesis "The dog is man's best friend." Everyone knows that already. Even the dog lovers will be uninterested, convinced they know better than you. But the cat . . . .

So it is with any unpopular idea. The more unpopular the viewpoint and the stronger the push against convention, the stronger the thesis and the more energetic the essay. Compare the energy in "Democracy is good" with that in "Communism is good," for instance. The first is filled with platitudes, the second with plutonium. By the same token, if you can find the real energy in "Democracy is good," if you can get down through the sand to where the roots and water are, you will have a real essay, because the opposition against which you generate your energy is the heaviest in the world: boredom. Probably the most energetic thesis of all, the greatest inner organizer, is some tired old truth that you cause to jet with new life, making the old ground green again.

To find a thesis and to put it into one sentence is to narrow and define your subject to a workable size. Under "Cats" you must deal with all felinity from the jungle up, carefully partitioning the eons and areas, the tigers and tabbies, the sizes and shapes. The minute you proclaim the cat the friend of man, you have pared away whole categories and chapters, and need only think up the arguments sufficient to overwhelm the opposition. So, put an argumentative edge on your subject—and you will have found your thesis.

Simple exposition, to be sure, has its uses. You may want to tell someone how to build a doghouse, how to can asparagus, how to follow the outlines of relativity, or even how to write an essay. Performing a few exercises in simple exposition will no doubt sharpen your insight into the problems of finding orderly sequences, of considering how best to lead your readers through the hoops, of writing clearly and accurately. It will also illustrate how much finer and surer an argument is.

You will see that picking an argument immediately simplifies the problems so troublesome in straight exposition: the defining, the partitioning, the narrowing of the subject. Actually, you can put an argumentative edge on the dullest of expository subjects. "How to build a doghouse" might become "Building a doghouse is a thorough introduction to the building trades, including architecture and mechanical engineering." "Canning asparagus" might become "An asparagus patch is a course in economics." "Relativity" might become "Relativity is not so inscrutable as many suppose." You have simply assumed that you have a loyal opposition consisting of the uninformed, the scornful, or both. You have given your subject its edge; you have limited and organized it at a single stroke. Pick an argument, then, and you will automatically be defining and narrowing your subject, and all the partitions that you don't need will fold up. Instead of dealing with things, subjects, and pieces of subjects, you will be dealing with an idea and its consequences.

Sharpen your thesis.

Come out with your subject pointed. Take a stand, make a judgment of value. Be reasonable, but don't be timid. It is helpful to think of your thesis, your main idea, as a debating question—"Resolved: Old-age pensions must go"—taking out the "Resolved" when you actually write the subject down. But your resolution will be even stronger, your essay clearer and tighter, if you can sharpen your thesis even further—"Resolved: Old-age pensions must go because _____." Fill in that blank and your worries are practically over. The main idea is to put your whole argument into one sentence.

Try, for instance: "Old-age pensions must go because they are making people irresponsible." I don't know at all if that is true, and neither will you until you write your way into it, considering probabilities and alternatives and objections, and especially the underlying assumptions. In fact, no one, no master sociologist or future historian, can tell absolutely if it is true, so multiplex are the causes in human affairs, so endless and tangled the consequences. The basic assumption—that irresponsibility is growing—may be entirely false. No one, I repeat, can tell absolutely. But for the same reason, your guess may be as good as another's. At any rate, you are now ready to write. You have found your *logos.*

Now you can put your well-pointed thesis sentence on a card on the wall in front of you to keep from drifting off target. But you will now want to dress it for the public, to burnish it and make it comely. Suppose you try:

> **Old-age pensions, perhaps more than anything else, are eroding our heritage of personal and familial responsibility.**

But is this true? Perhaps you had better try something like:

> **Despite their many advantages, old-age pensions may actually be eroding our heritage of personal and familial responsibility.**

This is really your thesis, and you can write that down on a scrap of paper too.

Believe in your thesis.

Notice how your original assertion has mellowed. And not because you have resorted to cheap tactics, though tactics may get a man to the same place, but rather because you have brought it under critical inspection. You have asked yourself what is true in it: what can (and cannot) be assumed true, what can (and cannot) be proved true. And you have asked yourself where you stand.

You should, indeed, look for a thesis you believe in, something you can even get enthusiastic about. Arguing on both sides of a question, as debaters do, is no doubt good exercise, if one can stand it. It breaks up old ground and uncovers what you can and do believe, at least for the moment. But the argument without the belief will be hollow. You can hardly persuade anyone if you can't persuade yourself. So begin with what you believe, and explore its validities.

Conversely, you must test your belief with all the objections you can think of, just as you have already tested your first proposition about old-age pensions. First, you have acknowledged the most evident objection—that the opposition's view must have some merit—by starting your final version with "Despite their many advantages . . . ." Second, you have gone a little deeper by seeing that in your bold previous version you had, with the words *are eroding*, begged the question of whether responsibility is in fact undergoing erosion; that is, you had silently assumed that responsibility *is* being eroded. This is one of the oldest fallacies and tricks of logic. To "beg the question," by error or intent, is to take for granted that which the opposition has not granted, to assume as already proved that which is yet to be proved. But you have saved yourself. You have changed *are eroding* to *may be eroding*. You have gone further in deleting the *perhaps more than anything else*. You have come closer to the truth.

Truth, for many, is something mystical and awesome; for others, something remote and impractical. And you may wonder if it is not astoundingly presumptuous to go around stating theses before you have studied your subject from all angles, made several house-to-house surveys, and read everything ever written. A natural uncertainty and feeling of ignorance, and a misunderstanding of what truth is, can well inhibit you from finding a thesis. But no one knows everything. No one would write anything if he waited until he did. To a great extent, as I have already said, the writing of a thing is the learning of it. This is why writing is so important: *it creates your own ideas,* as you try to find what you know and believe, and to convince others as well.

So, first, make a desperate thesis and get into the arena. This is probably solution enough. If it becomes increasingly clear that your thesis is untrue, no matter how hard you push it, turn it around and use the other end. If your convictions have begun to falter with:

Despite their many advantages, old-age pensions undermine responsibility . . . ,

try it the other way around, with something like:

Although old-age pensions may offend the rugged individualist, they relieve much want and anxiety, and they dispel much familial resentment.

You will now have a beautiful command of all the objections to your new position. And you will have learned something about human fallibility and the nature of truth.

We *are* fallible. Furthermore, the truth about our most teasing and insistent questions usually lies somewhere beyond our fingertips. You may know, or guess, the truth; you may believe that such-and-such is so. But often you can never know it or prove it in any physical way. And neither can anyone else. You can only take it on faith—as much faith as your temperament allows.

Differences of opinion, it is said, make a horse race, and we often hear that one man's opinion is as good as another's. But the race rather quickly proves that one man's opinion was wrong. There is no proof at all, however, of the opinion that Man O' War is the greatest three-year-old of all time. "All time" is a long time. All the returns are not yet in. And much of the past is beyond reach. But even this opinion, though we can never know for certain, is either right or wrong. All we can do is to weigh the probabilities, and believe.

Persuade your reader.

Once you believe in your proposition, you will discover that proving it is really a venture in persuasion. You have made a thesis, a hypothesis really—an opinion as to what the truth seems to be from where you stand, with the information you have. Oddly enough, your proof has nothing to do with *making* that opinion right or wrong. If it is right, it is right; if wrong, wrong—with or without proof. Your thesis is not "more right" after you have backed it with proof: it is merely shown to have been right all the time. Whether you got it in a flash or in a year's careful analysis makes no difference. You knew it from the moment of your conviction; now the skeptical reader must believe it too. You must give him enough evidence to persuade him that what you say is probably true, finding arguments that will stand up in the marketplace and survive the public haggle. You must find public reasons for your private convictions.

Don't apologize.

"In my opinion," the beginner will write repeatedly,· until he seems to be saying "It is only *my* opinion, after all, so it can't be worth much." He has failed to realize that his whole essay represents his opinion—of what the truth of the matter is. Don't make your essay a letter to Diary, or to Mother, or to Teacher, a confidential report of what happened to you last night as you agonized upon a certain question. "*To me,* Robert Frost is a great poet"—this is really writing about yourself. You are only confessing private convictions. To find the "public reasons" often requires no more than a trick of grammar: a shift from "*To me,* Robert Frost is . . ." to "Robert Frost is . . . ," from "*I thought* the book was good" to "The book is good," from you and your room last night to your subject and what it *is*. The grammatical shift represents a whole change of viewpoint, a shift from self to subject. You become the man of reason, showing the reader around firmly, politely, and persuasively.

Once you have effaced yourself from your thesis, once you have erased *to me* and *in my opinion* and all such signs of amateur terror, you may later let yourself back into the essay for emphasis of graciousness. "Mr. Watson, I think, is wrong." You can thus ease your most tentative or violent assertions, and show that you are polite and sensible, reasonably sure of your position but aware of the possibility of error. Again: the man of reason. But it is better to omit the "I" altogether than to write a junior autobiography of your discoveries and doubts.

Now, with clear conscience, you are ready to write. Your single thesis sentence has magically conjured up your essay. All you need now is some form to put it in.

Exercises

1. Convert each of the following general subjects into a debating resolution ("Resolved: Cats make better pets than dogs"; "Resolved: Old-age pensions must go"):

tropical fish	foreign languages
marijuana	abortion
violence	badminton
fraternities	the inner city
grades	stamps
the draft	communes
teen-agers	books

2. Pick three from your list of debating resolutions; drop the "Resolved"; and add a "because _____" ("Old-age pensions must go because they are making people irresponsible").

3. Now smooth out these three theses for public appearance, omitting the direct statement of *because,* and adding qualifications ("Despite their many advantages, old-age pensions may actually be eroding our heritage of personal and familial responsibility").

4. Now turn your three smoothed theses completely around, so that they assert the opposite ("Although old-age pensions may offend the rugged individualist, they relieve much want and anxiety, and they dispel much familial resentment").

2
Structure

Beginning, Middle, and End

Build your essay in three parts. There really is no other way. As Aristotle long ago pointed out, works that spin their way along through time need a beginning, a middle, and an end to give them the stability of spatial things like paintings and statues. You need a clear beginning to give your essay character and direction so the reader can tell where he is going and can look forward with expectation. Your beginning, of course, will set forth your thesis. You need a middle to amplify and fulfill. This will be the body of your argument. You need an end to let the reader know that he has arrived and where. This will be your final paragraph, a summation and reassertion of your theme.

Give your essay the three-part *feel* of beginning, middle, and end. The mind likes this triple order. Three has always been a magic number. The woodcutter always has three sons or three daughters; even the physical universe has three dimensions. Three has a basic psychological appeal as strong as a triangle or pyramid—especially with words and music, which the mind must pick up out of the air and assemble for itself into something like a spatial structure, a total impression. Many a freshman's essay has no structure and leaves no impression. It is all chaotic middle. It has no beginning, it just begins; it has no end, it just stops, fagged out at two in the morning.

The beginning must feel like a beginning, not like an accident. It should be a full paragraph that lets your reader gently into the subject and culminates with your thesis. The end, likewise, should be a full paragraph, one that drives the point home, pushes the implications wide, and brings the reader to rest, back on middle C, giving a sense of completion with the tonic. The next chapter describes the beginning and end paragraphs more fully. The "middle" of your essay, which constitutes its bulk, needs further structural consideration now.

Middle Tactics

Arrange your points in order of increasing interest.

Once your thesis has sounded the challenge, your reader's interest is probably at its highest pitch. He wants to see how you can prove so outrageous a thing, or to see what the arguments are for this thing he has always believed but never tested. Each step of the way into your demonstration, he is learning more of what you have to say. But, unfortunately, his interest may be relaxing as it becomes satisfied: the reader's normal line of attention is a progressive decline, arching down like a wintry graph. Against this decline you must oppose your forces, making each successive point more interesting, so that the vector of your reader's interest will continue at least on the horizontal, with no sag, and preferably with an upward swing:

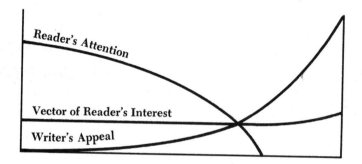

This is the basic principle for organizing the middle of your essay. Save your best till last. It is as simple as that.

Each successive item of your presentation should be more interesting than the last, or you will suddenly seem anticlimactic. Actually, minor regressions of interest make no difference so long as the whole tendency is uphill and your last item clearly the best. Suppose, for example, you were to undertake the cat thesis. You decide that four points would make up the case, and that you might arrange them in the following order of increasing interest: (1) cats are affectionate but make few demands; (2) cats actually look out for themselves; (3) cats have, in fact, proved extremely useful to man throughout history in controlling mice and other plaguey rodents; (4) cats satisfy some basic need in man for a touch of the jungle, savagery in repose, ferocity in silk, and have been worshiped for the exotic power they still seem to represent, even dozing on the banister. You may find, as you write, thinking up things, that Number 1 is developing attractive or amusing instances, and perhaps even virtually usurping the whole essay. Numbers 2, 3, and 4 should then be moved ahead as interesting but brief preliminaries. Your middle structure, thus, should range from least important to most important, from simple to complex, from narrow to broad, from pleasant to hilarious, from mundane to metaphysical—whatever "leasts" and "mosts" your subject suggests.

Acknowledge and dispose of the opposition.

Your cat essay, because it is moderately playful, can proceed rather directly, throwing only an occasional bone of concession to the dogs. But a serious controversial argument demands one organizational consideration beyond the simple structure of ascending interest. Although you have taken your stand firmly as a *pro*, you will have to allow scope to the *con's*, or you will seem not to have thought much about your subject. The more opposition you can manage as you carry your point, the more triumphant you will seem, like a man on a high wire daring the impossible.

The basic organizing principle here is to get rid of the opposition first, and to end on your own side. Probably you will have already organized your thesis sentence in a perfect pattern for your *con-pro* argument:

Despite their many advantages, old-age pensions . . . .
Although dogs are fine pets, cats . . . .

The subordinate clause states the subordinate part of your argument, which is your concession to the *con* viewpoint; your main clause states your main argument. As the subordinate clause comes first in your thesis sentence, so with the subordinate argument in your essay. Sentence and essay both reflect a natural psychological principle. You want, and the reader wants, to get the boys off the street so the men can have room. And you want to end on your best foot. (You might try putting the opposition last, just to see how peculiarly the last word insists on seeming best, and how, when stated last by you, the opposition's case seems to be your own.)

Get rid of the opposition first. This is the essential middle tactic of argumentation. If the opposing arguments seem relatively slight and brief, you can get rid of them all together in one paragraph before you get down to your case. Immediately after your beginning, which has stated your thesis, you write a paragraph of concession: "Of course, security is a good thing. No one wants old people begging." And so on to the end of the paragraph, deflating every conceivable objection. Then back to the main line: "But the price in moral decay is too great." The structure might be diagramed something like this:

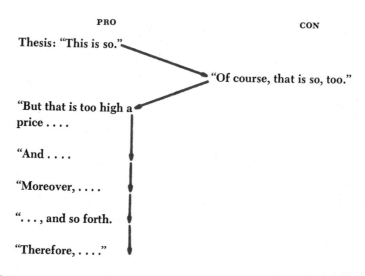

PRO   CON

Thesis: "This is so."

"Of course, that is so, too."

"But that is too high a price . . . .

"And . . . .

"Moreover, ...

". . . , and so forth.

"Therefore, ..."

If the opposition is more considerable, demolish it point by point, using a series of *con*'s and *pro*'s, in two or three paragraphs, before you steady down to your own side. Each paragraph can be a small argument that presents the opposition, then knocks it flat—a kind of Punch-and-Judy show: "We must admit that . . . . But . . . ." And down goes the poor old opposition again. Or you could swing your argument through a number of alternating paragraphs: first your beginning funnel and thesis, then a paragraph to the opposition (*con*), then one for your side (*pro*), then another paragraph of *con*, and so on. The main point, again, is this: get rid of the opposition first. One paragraph of concession right after your thesis will probably handle most of your adversaries, and the more complicated argumentative swingers, like the one diagramed on the facing page, will develop naturally as you need them.

You will notice that *but* and *however* are always guides for the *pro*'s, serving as switches back to the main line. *But, however,* and *Nevertheless* are the basic *pro*'s. *But* always heads its turning sentence (not followed by a comma); *Nevertheless* usually does (followed by a comma). I am sure, however, that *however* is always better buried in the sentence between commas. "However, . . . " is the habit of heavy prose. *But* is for the quick turn; the inlaid *however* for the more elegant sweep.

The structural line of your argument might look like this:

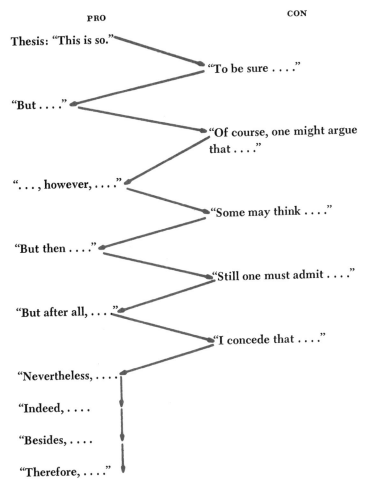

PRO

Thesis: "This is so."

"But . . . ."

". . . , however, ..."

"But then . . . ."

"But after all, . . ."

"Nevertheless, ..."

"Indeed, ...

"Besides, ...

"Therefore, ..."

CON

"To be sure . . . ."

"Of course, one might argue that . . . ."

"Some may think . . . ."

"Still one must admit . . . ."

"I concede that . . . ."

Run comparisons point by point.

After blasting the opposition first, only one argumentative principle remains: *run your comparisons point by point.* Don't write all about sheep for three pages, then all about goats. Every time you say something about a sheep, say something comparable about a goat, pelt for pelt, horn for horn, beard for beard. Otherwise your essay will fall in two, and you will need to repeat all your sheep points when you get down to goats, and at last begin the comparison. The tendency to organize comparisons by halves is so strong that you will probably find you have fallen into it unawares, and in rewriting you will have to reorganize everything point for point—still arranging your pairs of points from least important to most. Finally, the only comparison worth making is one that aims to demonstrate a superiority, one, that is, with a thesis—"Resolved: Sheep are more useful than goats."

Now you have almost finished your essay. You have found a thesis. You have worked it into a decent beginning. You have then worked out a convincing middle, with your arguments presented in a sequence of ascending interest; you have used up all your points and said your say. You and your argument are both exhausted. But don't stop. You need an end, or the whole thing will unravel in your reader's mind. You need to buttonhole him in a final paragraph, to imply "I told you so" without saying it, to hint at the whole round experience he has just had, and to leave him convinced, satisfied, and admiring. One more paragraph will do it: beginning, middle, *and* end.

Exercises

1. Write three *con*-and-*pro* thesis sentences, beginning "Although . . . ."

2. Write a five-hundred-word description of a process you know well—how to organize a demonstration, how to make a bracelet, a candle, a belt, a cake, how an internal combustion engine works. This is straight exposition. It will introduce you to the fine dry air of objectivity; to the problem of laying out in orderly sequence, for the reader's gathering comprehension, details that are in fact simultaneous; and to the difficulty of finding the clear, accurate, and descriptive phrase.

3. Now find a thesis that will change this description into an argument making some statement *about* the subject: organizing a demonstration requires a head for detail; making a cake is no child's play; what's under the hood is really no mystery. Rewrite the first paper using your new thesis and using, in some way, everything you said before.

4. Write a three-paragraph argumentative essay, conveying a thorough sense of beginning, middle, and end. (One of the best stylists I know, a German, told me that his grasp of organization comes from having had to write, through a number of grammar-school years, nothing but three-paragraph essays. The treatment appears to have been excellent.)

5. Take a popular proposition, like "Grades are unnecessary," "Marijuana should be legalized," or "Throw-away bottles should be abolished," and write down three or four supporting arguments, ones that would really stick. Arrange your items in order of increasing interest.

6. Choose a thesis to cover the following points (for or against public transportation, for instance). Then, underneath your thesis, list these points in an order of ascending interest, and in a *pro-con* structure, adding necessary *but*'s and *of course*'s and so forth, and other intermediate points of your own:

The automobile pollutes the atmosphere.
Public transportation is going bankrupt.
The economy requires obsolescence.
Cars were once built to last.
A car is a necessity.

7. Write an outline of a comparative argument. State your thesis; then simply list your points in order of increasing interest, phrasing them in the general pattern of "Painting is fun, but sculpture is better."

3
Paragraphs

The Standard Paragraph

A paragraph is a structural convenience—a building block to get firmly in mind. I mean the standard, central paragraph, setting aside for the moment the peculiarly shaped beginning paragraph and ending paragraph. You build the bulk of your essay with standard paragraphs, with blocks of concrete ideas, and they must fit smoothly. But they must also remain as perceptible parts, to rest your reader's eye and mind. Indeed, the paragraph originated, among the Greeks, as a resting place and place finder, being first a mere mark (*graphos*) in the margin alongside (*para*) an unbroken sheet of handwriting—the proofreader's familiar ¶. You have heard that a paragraph is a single idea, and this is true. But so is a word, usually; and so is a sentence, sometimes. It seems best, after all, to think of a paragraph as something you use for your reader's convenience, rather than as some granitic form laid down by molten logic.

The writing medium determines the size of the paragraph. Your average longhand paragraph may look the same size to you as a typewritten one, and both may seem the same size as a paragraph in a book. But the printed page might show your handwritten paragraph so short as to be embarrassing, and your typewritten paragraph barely long enough for decency. Handwriting plus typewriting plus insecurity equals inadequate paragraphs. Your first impulse may be to write little paragraphs, often only a sentence to each. If so, you are not yet writing in any medium at all.

Journalists, of course, are habitually one-sentence paragraphers. The narrowness of the newspaper column makes a sentence look like a paragraph, and narrow columns and short paragraphs serve the rapid transit for which newspapers are designed. A paragraph from a book might fill a whole newspaper column with solid lead. It would have to be broken—paragraphed—for the reader's convenience. On the other hand, a news story on the page of a book would look like a gap-toothed comb, and would have to be consolidated for the reader's comfort.

Plan for the big paragraph.

Imagine yourself writing for print, but in a book, not a newspaper. Force yourself to four or five sentences at least, visualizing your paragraphs as about all of a size. Think of them as identical rectangular frames to be filled. This will allow you to build with orderly blocks, to strengthen your feel for structure. Since the beginner's problem is usually one of thinking of things to say rather than of trimming the overgrowth, you can do your filling out a unit at a time, always thinking up one or two sentences more to fill the customary space. You will probably be repetitive and wordy at first—this is our universal failing —but you will soon learn to fill your paragraph with clean and interesting details. You will get to feel a kind of constructional rhythm as you find yourself coming to a resting place at the end of your customary paragraphic frame. Once accustomed to a five-sentence frame, say, you can then begin to vary the length for emphasis, letting a good idea swell out beyond the norm, or bringing a particular point home in a paragraph short and sharp.

Find a topic sentence.

Looked at as a convenient structural frame, the paragraph reveals a further advantage. Like the essay itself, it has a beginning, a middle, and an end. The beginning and the end are usually each one sentence long, and the middle gets you smoothly from one to the other. Since, like the essay, the paragraph flows through time, its last sentence is the most emphatic. This is your home punch. The first sentence holds the next most emphatic place. It will normally be your *topic sentence,* stating the small thesis of a miniature essay, something like this:

> *Jefferson believed in democracy because of his fearless belief in reason.* He knew that reason was far from perfect, but he also knew that it was the best faculty we have. He knew that it was better than all the frightened and angry intolerances with which we fence off our own back yards at the cost of injustice. Thought must be free. Discussion must be free. Reason must be free to range among the

widest possibilities. Even the opinion we hate, and have reasons for believing wrong, we must leave free so that reason can operate on it, so that we advertise our belief in reason and demonstrate a faith unafraid of the consequences—because we know that the consequences will be right. Freedom is really not the aim and end of Jeffersonian democracy: freedom is the means by which democracy can rationally choose justice for all.

If your topic sentence covers everything within your paragraph, you are using your paragraphs with maximum effect, leading your reader into your community block by block. If your end sentences bring him briefly to rest, he will know where he is and appreciate it.

Beginning Paragraphs: The Funnel

State your thesis at the END of your beginning paragraph.

Your beginning paragraph must contain your main idea, and present it to best advantage. Its topic sentence is also the *thesis sentence* of your entire essay. The clearest and most emphatic place for your thesis sentence is at the *end*—not at the beginning—of the beginning paragraph. If you put it first, you will have to repeat some version of it as you bring your beginning paragraph to a close. If you put it in the middle, the reader will very likely take something else as your main point, probably whatever the last sentence contains. The inevitable psychology of interest, as you move your reader through your first paragraph and into your essay, urges you to put your thesis last—in the last sentence of your beginning paragraph.

Think of your beginning paragraph, then, not as a frame to be filled, but as a funnel. Start wide and end narrow:

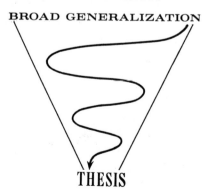

BROAD GENERALIZATION

THESIS

If, for instance, you wished to show that learning to play the guitar pays off in friendship, you would start some distance back from that point. You could start almost anywhere, but start somewhere back from your specific thesis with something more general—about music, about learning, about the pleasures of achievement, about guitars: "Playing the guitar looks easy," "Music can speak more directly than words," "Learning anything is a course in frustration." You can even open with something quite specific, *as long as it is more general than your thesis:* "Pick up a guitar, and you bump into people." Your opening line, in other words, should be something to engage interest easily, something to which most readers would assent without a rise in blood pressure. (Antagonize and startle if you wish, but beware of having the door slammed before you have a chance, and of making your thesis an anticlimax.) Therefore: broad and genial. From your opening geniality, you move progressively down to smaller particulars. You narrow down: from learning in general, to learning the guitar, to the guitar's musical and social complications, to its rewards in achievement, to rewards in friendship (your thesis). Your paragraph might run, from broad to narrow, like this:

> Learning anything has unexpected rocks in its path, but the guitar seems particularly rocky. It looks so simple. A few chords, you think, and you are on your way. Then you discover not only the musical and technical difficulties, but a whole unexpected crowd of human complications. Your friends think you are showing off; the people you meet think you are a fake. Then the frustrations drive you to achievement. You learn to face the music and the people honestly. You finally learn to play a little, but you also discover something better. You have learned to make and keep some real friends, because you have discovered a kind of ultimate friendship with yourself.

Now, that paragraph turned out a little different from what I anticipated. I overshot my original thesis, discovering, as I wrote, a thesis one step farther—an underlying cause—about coming to friendly terms with oneself. But it illustrates the funnel, from the broad and general to the one particular point that will be your essay's main idea, your thesis. Here is another example:

> The environment is the world around us, and everyone agrees it needs a cleaning. Big corporations gobble up the countryside and disgorge what's left into the breeze and streams. Big trucks rumble by, trailing their fumes. A jet roars into the air, and its soot drifts over

the trees. Everyone calls for massive action, and then tosses away his cigarette butt or gum wrapper. The world around us is also a sidewalk, a lawn, a lounge, a hallway, a room right here. Cleaning the environment can begin by reaching for the scrap of paper at your feet.

Middle Paragraphs

Make your middle paragraphs full, and use transitions.

The middle paragraph is the standard paragraph, the little essay in itself, with its own little beginning and little end. But it must also declare its allegiance to the paragraphs immediately before and after it. Each topic sentence must somehow hook onto the paragraph above it, must include some word or phrase to ease the reader's path: a transition. You may simply repeat a word from the sentence that ended the paragraph just above. You may bring down a thought left slightly hanging in air: "Smith's idea is different" might be a tremendously economical topic sentence with automatic transition. Or you may get from one paragraph to the next by the usual stepping-stones, like *but, however, nevertheless, therefore, indeed, of course.* One brief transitional touch in your topic sentence is usually sufficient.

The topic sentences in each of the following three paragraphs by James Baldwin contain neat transitions. I have just used an old standby myself: repeating the words *topic sentence* from the close of my preceding paragraph. Mr. Baldwin has just described the young people of Harlem who have given up, escaping into day-long TV, or the local bar, or drugs. He now begins his next paragraph with *And the others,* a strong and natural transition, referring back, reinforced with the further transitional reference *all these deaths.* In the next paragraph, *them* does the trick; in the last, *other* again makes the transition and sets the contrast. The paragraphs are nearly the same length, all cogent, clear, and full. No one-sentence paragraphing here, no gaps, but all a vivid, orderly progression:

> And the others, who have avoided all of these deaths, get up in the morning and go downtown to meet "the man." They work in the white man's world all day and come home in the evening to this fetid block. They struggle to instill in their children some private sense of honor or dignity which will help the child to survive. This means, of course, that they must struggle, stolidly, incessantly, to keep this sense alive in themselves, in spite of the insults, the indifference, and the cruelty they

are certain to encounter in their working day. They patiently browbeat the landlord into fixing the heat, the plaster, the plumbing; this demands prodigious patience; nor is patience usually enough. In trying to make their hovels habitable, they are perpetually throwing good money after bad. Such frustration, so long endured, is driving many strong, admirable men and women whose only crime is color to the very gates of paranoia.

One remembers them from another time—playing handball in the playground, going to church, wondering if they were going to be promoted at school. One remembers them going off to war—gladly, to escape this block. One remembers their return. Perhaps one remembers their wedding day. And one sees where the girl is now—vainly looking for salvation from some other embittered, trussed, and struggling boy —and sees the all-but-abandoned children in the streets.

Now I am perfectly aware that there are other slums in which white men are fighting for their lives, and mainly losing. I know that blood is also flowing through those streets and that the human damage there is incalculable. People are continually pointing out to me the wretchedness of white people in order to console me for the wretchedness of blacks. But an itemized account of the American failure does not console me and it should not console anyone else. That hundreds of thousands of white people are living, in effect, no better than the "niggers" is not a fact to be regarded with complacency. The social and moral bankruptcy suggested by this fact is of the bitterest, most terrifying kind.*

End Paragraphs: The Inverted Funnel

Reassert your thesis.

If the beginning paragraph is a funnel, the end paragraph is a funnel upside down: the thought starts moderately narrow—it is more or less the thesis you have had all the time—and then pours out broader and broader implications and finer emphases. The end paragraph reiterates, summarizes, and emphasizes with decorous fervor. This is your last chance. This is what your reader will carry away— and if you can carry *him* away, so much the better. All within decent intellectual bounds, of course. You are the man of reason still, but the man of reason supercharged with conviction, sure of his idea and sure of its importance.

---

* "Fifth Avenue Uptown: A Letter from Harlem," in *Nobody Knows My Name* (New York: Dial Press, 1961), pp. 59–61. Copyright © 1960 by James Baldwin. Reprinted by permission of Dial Press. (Originally published in *Esquire.*)

The last paragraph conveys a sense of assurance and repose, of business completed. Its topic sentence should be some version of your original thesis sentence, since the end paragraph is the exact structural opposite and complement of the beginning one. Its transitional word or phrase is often one of finality or summary—*then, finally, thus,* and *so:*

> So the guitar is a means to a finer end.
> The environment, then, is in our lungs and at our fingertips.

The paragraph would then proceed to expand and elaborate this revived thesis. We would get a confident assertion that both the music and the friendships are really by-products of an inner alliance; we would get an urgent plea to clean up our personal environs and strengthen our convictions. One rule of thumb: the longer the paper, the more specific the summary of the points you have made. A short paper will need no specific summary of your points at all; the renewed thesis and its widening of implications are sufficient.

Here is an end paragraph by Sir James Jeans. His transitional phrase is *for a similar reason.* His thesis was that previous concepts of physical reality had mistaken surfaces for depths:

> The purely mechanical picture of visible nature fails for a similar reason. It proclaims that the ripples themselves direct the workings of the universe instead of being mere symptoms of occurrences below; in brief, it makes the mistake of thinking that the weather-vane determines the direction from which the wind shall blow, or that the thermometer keeps the room hot.[*]

Here is an end paragraph by Charles Wyzanski, Jr. His transitional phrase is *Each generation,* since he has been talking of the perpetual gap. His thesis was that differences, including those between generations, have stimulated life to higher modes:

> Each generation is faced with a challenge of making some kind of sense out of its existence. In advance, it knows from the Book of Job and the Book of Ecclesiastes and the Greek drama that there will be no right answer. But there will be forms of answer. There will be a style. As ancient Greece had the vision of *arete* (the noble warrior), as Dante and the Medievalists had the vision of the great and universal Catholic Church, even as the founding fathers of the American Republic had the vision of the new order which they began, so for the young the question is to devise a style—not one that will be good

---

[*] *The New Background of Science* (Cambridge: Cambridge University Press, 1933), p. 261.

semper et ubique, but one for our place and our time, one that will be a challenge to the very best that is within our power of reach, and one that will make us realize, in Whitehead's immortal terms, that for us the only reality is the process. *

Here is an end paragraph of Professor Richard Hofstadter's. His transitional word is *intellectuals,* carried over from the preceding paragraphs. His thesis was that intellectuals should not abandon their defense of intellectual and spiritual freedom, as they have tended to do, under pressure to conform:

> This world will never be governed by intellectuals—it may rest assured. But *we* must be assured, too, that intellectuals will not be altogether governed by this world, that they maintain their piety, their longstanding allegiance to the world of spiritual values to which they should belong. Otherwise there will be no intellectuals, at least not above ground. And societies in which the intellectuals have been driven underground, as we have had occasion to see in our own time, are societies in which even the anti-intellectuals are unhappy.†

The Whole Essay

You have now discovered the main ingredients of a good essay. You have learned to find and to sharpen your thesis in one sentence, to give your essay that all-important argumentative edge. You have learned to arrange your points in order of increasing interest, and you have practiced disposing of the opposition in a *pro-con* structure. You have seen that your beginning paragraph should look like a funnel, working from broad generalization to thesis. You have tried your hand at middle paragraphs, which are almost like little essays with their own beginnings and ends. And finally, you have learned that your last paragraph should work like an inverted funnel, broadening and embellishing your thesis.

Some students have pictured the essay as a Greek column, with a narrowing beginning paragraph as its top, or capital, and a broadening end paragraph as its base. Others have seen it as a keyhole,‡ which is

---

* "A Federal Judge Digs the Young," *Saturday Review,* July 20, 1968, p. 62.

† "Democracy and Anti-intellectualism in America," *Michigan Quarterly Review,* 59 (1953), 295.

‡ Mrs. Fran Measley of Santa Barbara, California, has devised for her students a mimeographed sheet to accompany my discussion of structure and paragraphing —to help them to visualize my points, through a keyhole, as it were. I am grateful to Mrs. Measley to be able to include it here.

the visualization I prefer (see the diagram opposite). But either way, you should see a structure, with solid beginning and end, supported by a well-shaped middle. The student's essay that follows illustrates this structure. The assignment had asked for about five hundred words on some book (or movie, or TV program, or event) that had proved personally meaningful. The essay is a little wordy, a little uncertain in its language and unfocused in thesis. The author has not yet fully discovered her own written voice. But it is an excellent start, and a nice illustration of the essay's basic structure: beginning, middle, and end.

On Growing Up

Reading for pleasure is not considered to be popular. Young adults prefer the "boob tube," the television set with which they have spent so many childhood hours. Too many attractions beckon them away from the books that the teacher recommended to the class for summer reading. One's friends come by in their automobiles to drive down for a coke. The kids go to the moving pictures, or to the beach, and the book one had intended to read remains on the shelf, or probably in the library, where one has not yet been able to find the time to go. Nevertheless, a book can furnish real enjoyment.

The reader enjoys the experience of being in another world. While he reads, he forgets that he is in his own room. The book has served as a magic carpet to transport him to India, or Africa, or Sweden, or even to the cities and areas of his own country where he has never been. It has also transported him into the lives of people with different experiences and problems, from which he can learn to solve his own problems of the future. The young person, in particular, can learn by the experience of reading what it is like to be a complete adult.

A book is able to help the young person to mature even further, and change his whole point of view. *Growing Up in New Guinea* by Margaret Mead is a valuable experience for this reason. I found the book on our shelf, after having seen Margaret Mead on TV. I was interested in her because the teacher had referred to her book entitled *Coming of Age in Samoa*. I was surprised to find this one about New Guinea. I thought it was a mistake. I opened it and read the first sentence: "The way in which each human infant is transformed into the finished adult, into the complicated individual version of his city and his century, is one of the most fascinating studies open to the curious minded." The idea that the individual is a version of his city and his century was fascinating. I started reading and was surprised when I was called to dinner to learn that two hours had passed. I could hardly eat my dinner fast enough so that I could get back to New Guinea.

THE KEYHOLE

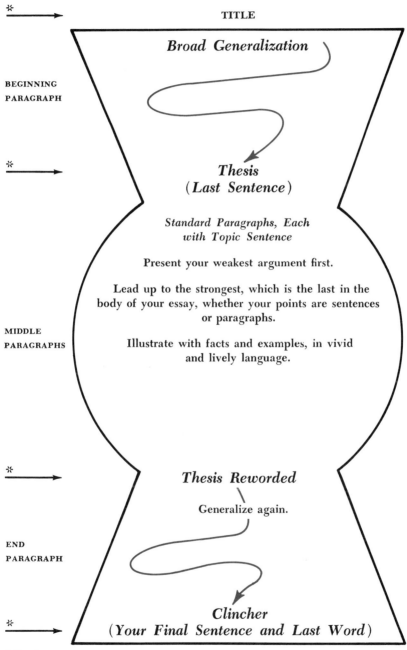

TITLE

Broad Generalization

BEGINNING
PARAGRAPH

Thesis
(*Last Sentence*)

*Standard Paragraphs, Each
with Topic Sentence*

Present your weakest argument first.

Lead up to the strongest, which is the last in the
body of your essay, whether your points are sentences
or paragraphs.

Illustrate with facts and examples, in vivid
and lively language.

MIDDLE
PARAGRAPHS

Thesis Reworded

Generalize again.

END
PARAGRAPH

Clincher
(*Your Final Sentence and Last Word*)

* Focal points

From this book, I learned that different cultures have very different conceptions about what is right and wrong, in particular about the sex relations and the marriage ceremony, but that people have the same problems all over the world, namely, the problem of growing up. I also learned that books can be more enjoyable than any other form of pleasure. Books fascinate the reader because while he is learning about other people and their problems, particularly about the problem of growing up, he is also learning about his own problems.

Exercises

1. Write three beginning paragraphs of five or six sentences each, working down in each to some such terse thesis as one of these: "Without health there is nothing." "Reason is best." "Everything is relative." "Always prepare for the worst." "Live for the day." "Worry is good."

2. Write five topic sentences for end paragraphs, each with a different transitional tag, as in these examples: "Ill health, *then,* darkens every prospect and discolors every thought." "It is clear, *therefore,* that ill health has produced more truth and more beauty—more art, more literature, more music, and a good share of philosophy, history, invention, and scientific insight—than have all the muscles in all outdoors." "One can, *in the last analysis,* live only the present moment."

3. Write an end paragraph to go with each of the two beginning paragraphs on pages 19–20.

4. Write a beginning paragraph, and top it with a title for the essay, to go with each of the three end paragraphs on pages 22–23.

5. Write three middle paragraphs, about 200 words each, on different subjects. Make the topic sentences cover the contents, and give each topic sentence some transitional touch: "Fly fishing *is different.*" "*But* Judaism acknowledges man as a social being." "Kennedy *also* had his blind side."

6. Write an essay with uniform paragraphs, each about 125 words long, each, after a good beginning paragraph with a thesis, having a good sharp topic sentence—and don't forget the end.

7. Write a three-paragraph essay, then expand it into a five-paragraph essay, keeping the same beginning paragraph and end paragraph, and hand in both versions.

4
Evidence

Now with the whole essay in hand, we need just a little more thought. We need to check the evidence. Have you brought in enough to prove your point? Have you bored your reader with too much? Where can it go wrong? And what is evidence anyway?

Use specific examples.

Evidence is simply an example, something specific to illustrate your general thesis. And your thesis itself will suggest what examples you need. To support a thesis that pensions breed irresponsibility, you describe an irresponsible pensioner—one you know. To illustrate that a character in a novel is unbelievable, you describe the inconsistencies you noticed in him when you read it. To show that violent crimes are increasing, you bring in the statistics you have seen in the newspaper, and perhaps a recent murder or two, and a statement from the chief of police: evidence you would have noticed before you thought to form it into a thesis. Your thesis, your big idea, has emerged from the specific things you have seen, in person, in print, or on TV. Now you use them to support your thesis in turn. Make them brief, but sufficient. Three, as always, is an ideal number.

Several examples are always better than one. One, all alone, implies a universal typicality it may not have. It raises the nagging problem you have already worked at in developing your thesis and its contraries: the problem of unexamined assumptions, which lies behind all fallacies in logic, the mistake of assuming inadvertently that *one,* or *some,* equals *all.*

Check your assumptions.

Ask yourself, again, if your essay hangs on some unsuspected assumption. Suppose you have said that football builds character. As evidence, you have told how going out for practice has transformed a happy-go-lucky youth into a disciplined man with a part-time job and good grades. But you have assumed, without thinking, that nothing else would have worked as well, that football would work every time, that character consists only in self-discipline, and perhaps that women have no character at all. Your evidence is persuasive, but the hidden assumptions need resurfacing.

First, limit your assumptions by narrowing your thesis:

Although no magical guarantee, football strengthens the rugged and disciplined side of character.

You then concede that some football players are downright wild, and that character includes social responsibility, moral courage, intelligence, compassion. (You can then probably claim some of these back for football too.) Then bring in some more examples. Three different young players, who have matured in different ways, would strengthen your point, and would assume only reasonable virtues for pigskin and practice.

Check your authorities.

We reasonably assume that authorities are right. What they say—about population, pollution, economics, tooth decay—is indeed most persuasive evidence. Use them. Quote them directly, if you can, and put your source in a footnote:

According to Freud, establishing the ego is a kind of "reclamation work, like the draining of the Zuyder Zee."[1]

[1] *New Introductory Lectures on Psycho-Analysis,* trans. W. J. H. Sprott (New York: W. W. Norton & Co., 1933), p. 112.
[Note that I omit the author's name in the footnote because I have already named him in my text, which is the best place. Note also that I have quoted the shortest possible segment of Freud's sentence to get the sharpest focus, and that I have run it into my own sentence within quotation marks. You would indent and single-space a long quotation, and omit the quotation marks: for further details see, pp. 74–75, 104.]

An indirect reference, footnoted, works as well:

Freud likens psychotherapy to reclaiming territory from the sea.[1]

The mere name of a Freud, an Einstein, or a Shakespeare can touch your paper with power.

But citing an authority risks four common fallacies. The first is in appealing to the authority outside of his field, even if his field is the universe. Although Einstein was a man of powerful intellect, we should not assume he knew all about women too. The second fallacy is in misrepresenting what the authority really says. Sir Arthur Eddington (I cite an authority myself) puts the case: "It is a common mistake to suppose that Einstein's theory of relativity asserts that everything is relative. Actually it says, 'There are absolute things in the world but you must look deeply for them. The things that first present themselves to your notice are for the most part relative.'"* If you appeal loosely to Einstein to show that "everything is relative," you have misrepresented his theory. The third fallacy is in assuming that one instance from an authority represents him accurately. In one place, Shakespeare calls women fiends; in another, angels. The fourth fallacy is deepest: the authority may have faded. New facts have generated new ideas. Einstein has limited Newton's authority. Geology and radioactive carbon have challenged the authority of Genesis. So ask these four questions:

1. Am I citing this authority outside his field?
2. Am I presenting him accurately?
3. Is this instance really representative?
4. Is he still fully authoritative?

Do not claim too much for him, and add other kinds of proof, preferably an example you yourself have seen. In short, don't put all your eggs in one basket.

Check your conclusions.

What you conclude from your evidence is equally open to question. So question yourself, before your final draft. Put your faith in probability. If you say, "Apples are good food," you assume boldly that all apples are good, and you are not upset by the bad one in the barrel. You know that bad apples are neither so numerous nor so typical that you must conclude, "Apples are unfit for human consumption." You also know what causes the bad ones. So see that probability supports your generalization by checking the following conditions:

1. Your samples are reasonably numerous.
2. Your samples are truly typical.
3. Your exceptions are explainable, and demonstrably not typical.

---

* *The Nature of the Physical World* (Ann Arbor: University of Michigan Press, 1958), p. 23.

Question, especially, your statistics. They can deceive badly because they look so solid—especially averages and percentages. "The average student earns ten dollars a week" may conceal the truth that one earns a hundred dollars and nine earn nothing. And a sample of ten students hardly represents thirty thousand. Moreover, each "one" in any statistical count represents a slightly different quantity, as a glance around a class of twenty students makes clear. So use your statistics with understanding, preferably with other specific examples.

Then, finally, ask if your evidence might not support some other conclusion. Some linguists, for example, have concluded that speech is superior to writing because speech has more "signals" than writing. But from the same evidence one might declare speech inferior: writing conveys the same message with fewer signals.

In the end, your evidence depends on common sense. Don't assume that one swallow makes a summer, and also check your generalizations for the following fallacies:

1. *Either-or.* You assume only two opposing possibilities: "either we abolish requirements or education is finished." Education will probably amble on, somewhere in between.

2. *Oversimplification.* As with *either-or*, you ignore alternatives. "A student learns only what he wants to learn" ignores all the pressures from parents and society, which in fact account for a good deal of learning.

3. *Begging the question.* A somewhat unhandy term, which we have already seen (p. 5): you assume as proved something that really needs proving. "Free all political prisoners" assumes that none of those concerned has committed an actual crime.

4. *Ignoring the question.* The question of whether it is right for a neighborhood to organize against a newcomer shifts to land values and taxes.

5. *Non sequitur.* ("It does not follow.") "He's certainly sincere; he must be right." "He's the most popular; he should be president." The conclusions do not reasonably follow from sincerity and popularity.

6. *Post hoc, ergo propter hoc.* ("After this, therefore because of this.") The non sequitur of events: "He stayed up late and therefore won the race." He probably won in spite of late hours, and for other reasons.

Exercises

1. Write three assertions based on imperfect assumptions ("Football builds character"), explaining the imperfections briefly under each sentence.

2. Write some crisp examples (no more than one or two sentences each) to illustrate three of the following assertions:

(a) Football strengthens the rugged and disciplined side of character.

(b) Good writing comes more from work than from inspiration.

(c) Shakespeare (or any other writer you know) uses vivid figures of speech.

(d) Required courses are not all bad.

(e) Much education occurs outside the classroom.

3. For each of the following quotations, make a sentence of your own that selects and quotes a well-focused part, and give it a proper footnote.

(a) Writing indeed has a certain mystery about it, just as life does. But the stylistic side of writing is, in fact, the only side that can be analyzed and learned.

    Sheridan Baker, *The Practical Stylist* (New York: Thomas Y. Crowell Co., 1973), p. 1.

(b) They struggle to instill in their children some private sense of honor or dignity which will help the child to survive. This means, of course, that they must struggle, stolidly, incessantly, to keep this sense alive in themselves, in spite of the insults, the indifference, and the cruelty they are certain to encounter in their working day.

    James Baldwin, "Fifth Avenue Uptown: A Letter from Harlem," in *Nobody Knows My Name* (New York: Dial Press, 1961), pp. 59–60.

(c) What a piece of work is a man! How noble in reason, how infinite in faculty. In form and moving, how express and admirable. In action, how like an angel; in apprehension, how like a god. The beauty of the world! The paragon of animals! And yet, to me, what is this quintessence of dust?

    William Shakespeare, *Hamlet* II.ii.315–321.

(d) Brokers said the market lacked stimulating news. Some investors were awaiting new signs of economic direction.

    New York Times, June 14, 1974, Sec. 4, p. 3.

4. Write a sentence illustrating each of the four faulty appeals to authority (pp. 28–29). In other words, write four bad examples.

5. Look through the newspaper for some statistics—about how many

people are killed by automobiles, airplanes, lung cancer, or what not. Write a paragraph suggesting the possibilities the figures do not represent (differences of age, deaths by other means, the usual death rate, and so forth).

6. Write a sentence to illustrate each of the six fallacies on page 30; add a note explaining the fallacy in each. In other words, make up some bad examples and explain what is wrong with them.

5
Writing Good Sentences

All this time you have been writing sentences, as naturally as breathing, and perhaps with as little variation. Now for a close look at the varieties of the sentence. Some varieties can be shaggy and tangled indeed. But they are all offshoots of the simple active sentence, the basic English genus *John hit Joe,* with action moving straight from subject through verb to object.

This subject-verb-object sentence can be infinitely grafted and contorted, but there are really only two general varieties of it: (1) the "loose, or strung-along," in Aristotle's phrase, and (2) the periodic. English naturally runs "loose." Our thoughts are by nature strung along from subject through verb to object, with whatever comes to mind simply added as it comes—a word order happily acquired from French as a result of the Norman Conquest. But we can also use the periodic sentence characteristic of our German and Latin ancestry, a sentence in which ideas hang in the air like girders until all interconnections are locked by the final word: *John, the best student in the class, the tallest and most handsome, hit Joe.*

So we have two varieties of the English sentence, partly because its old Germanic oak was first limbered by French and then cured by Latin, but mostly because (as Aristotle observed of Greek) the piece-by-piece and the periodic species simply represent two ways of thought: the first, the natural stringing of thoughts as they come; the second, the more careful contrivance of emphasis and suspense.

The Simple Sentence

Use the simple active sentence, loosely periodic.

Your best sentences will be hybrids of the loose and the periodic. First, learn to use active verbs (*John* HIT *Joe*), which will keep you within the simple active pattern with all parts showing (subject-verb-object), as opposed to verbs in the passive voice (*Joe* WAS HIT *by John*), which throw your sentences into the shade. Then learn to give your native strung-along sentence a touch of periodicity and suspense.

Any change in normal order can give you unusual emphasis, as when you move the object ahead of the subject:

> That I like.
> The house itself she hated, but the yard was grand.
> Nature I loved; and next to Nature, Art.
> The manuscript, especially, he treasured.

You can vary the subject-verb-object pattern more gently by inter-ruptive words and phrases, so that the meaning gathers excitement from the delay. The *especially* does more for the manuscript than the words themselves could manage: the phrase postpones the already postponed subject and predicate. Put the phrase last, and the emphasis fades considerably; the speaker grows a little remote: "The manuscript he treasured, especially." Put the sentence in normal order—"He especially treasured the manuscript"—and we are, in fact, back to normal.

We expect our ideas one at a time, in normal succession—*John hit Joe*—and with anything further added, in proper sequence, at the end —*a real haymaker*. Change this fixed way of thinking, and you im-mediately put your reader on the alert for something unusual. Conse-quently, some of your best sentences will be simple active ones sprung wide with phrases coloring subject, verb, object, or all three, in various ways. You may, for instance, effectively complicate the subject:

> King Lear, proud, old, and childish, probably aware that his grip on the kingdom is beginning to slip, devises a foolish plan.
> To come all this way, to arrive after dark, and then to find the place locked and black as ink was almost unbearable.

Or the verb:

> He made his way, carefully at first, then confidently, then with reck-less steps, along the peak of the smoldering roof.
> A good speech usually begins quietly, proceeds sensibly, gathers mo-mentum, and finally moves even the most indifferent audience.

Or the object:

> She finally wrote the paper, a long desperate perambulation without beginning or end, without any guiding idea—without, in fact, much of an idea at all.

His notebooks contain marvelous comments on the turtle in his back yard, the flowers and weeds, the great elm by the drive, the road, the earth, the stars, and the men and women of the village.

These are some of the infinite possibilities in the simple active sentence as it delays and stretches and heightens the ordinary expectations of subject-verb-object.

Compound and Complex Sentences

Learn the difference between compound and complex sentences.

You make a compound sentence by linking together simple sentences with a coordinating conjunction (*and, but, or, nor, yet*) or with a colon or a semicolon. You make a complex one by hooking lesser sentences onto the main sentence with *that, which, who,* or one of the many other subordinating connectives like *although, because, where, when, after, if.* The compound sentence *coordinates,* treating everything on the same level; the complex *subordinates,* putting everything else somewhere below its one main self-sufficient idea. The compound links ideas one after the other, as in the basic simple sentence; the complex is a simple sentence delayed and elaborated by clauses instead of merely by phrases. The compound represents the strung-along way of thinking; the complex represents the periodic.

Avoid simpleminded compounds.

Essentially the compound sentence *is* simpleminded, a set of clauses on a string—a child's description of a birthday party, for instance: "We got paper hats and we pinned the tail on the donkey and we had chocolate ice cream and Randy sat on a piece of cake and I won third prize." *And . . . and . . . and.*

But this way of thinking is necessary, even in postgraduate regions. It is always useful simply for pacing off related thoughts, and for breaking the staccato of simple statement. It often briskly connects cause and effect: "The clock struck one, and down he run." "The solipsist relates all knowledge to his own being, and the demonstrable commonwealth of human nature dissolves before his dogged timidity." The *and* can link causes with all sorts of different effects and speed, can bring in the next clause as a happy afterthought or a momentous

consequence. Since the compound sentence is built on the most enduring of colloquial patterns—the simple sequence of things said as
they occur to the mind—it has the pace, the immediacy, and the dramatic effect of talk. Hemingway, for instance, often gets all the numb
tension of a shell-shocked mind by reducing his character's thoughts
all to one level, in sentences something like this: "It was a good night
and I sat at a table and . . . and . . . and . . . ."

With *but* and *or,* the compound sentence becomes more thoughtful.
The mind is at work, turning its thought first one way, then another,
meeting the reader's objections by stating them. With semicolon and
colon (or, if the clauses are very short, with comma), the compound
grows more sophisticated still:

> John demands the most from himself; Pete demands.
> I came, I saw, I conquered.
> Economic theorists assume a common man: he commonly wants more
> than he can supply.

Think of the compound sentence in terms of its conjunctions—the
words that yoke its clauses—and of the accompanying punctuation.
Here are three basic groups of conjunctions that will help you sort out
and punctuate your compound thoughts.

Group I. The three common coordinating conjunctions: and, but,
and or (nor). *Put a comma before each.*

> I like her, and I don't mind saying so.
> Art is long, but life is short.
> Win this point, or the game is lost.

Group II. Conjunctive adverbs: therefore, moreover, however,
nevertheless, consequently, furthermore. *Put a semicolon before, a
comma after, each.*

> Nations indeed seem to have a kind of biological span like the ages
> of man himself, from rebellious youth, through caution, to decay;
> consequently, predictions of doom are not uncommon.

Group III. Some in-betweeners—yet, still, so—*which sometimes
take a comma, sometimes a semicolon, depending on your pace and
emphasis.*

> We long for the good old days, yet we never include the disadvantages.
> Man longs for the good old days; yet he rarely takes into account the
> inaccuracy of human memory.

The preparation had been halfhearted and hasty, so the meeting was wretched.

Rome declined into the pleasures of its circuses and couches; so the tough barbarians conquered.

Learn to subordinate.

You probably write compound sentences almost without thinking. But the subordinations of the complex usually require some thought. Indeed, you are ranking closely related thoughts, arranging the lesser ones so that they bear effectively on your main thought and clarify their connections to it. You must first pick your most important idea. You must then change the thoughtless *co*ordination of mere sequence into various forms of *sub*ordination—ordering your lesser thoughts "sub," or below, the main idea. The childish birthday-party sentence, then, might come out something like this:

> After paper hats and chocolate ice cream, after Randy's sitting on a piece of cake and everyone's pinning the tail on the donkey, I WON FIRST PRIZE.

You do the trick with connectives—with any word, like *after* in the sentence above, indicating time, place, cause, or other qualification:

> *If* he tries, *if* he fails, HE IS STILL GREAT *because* his spirit is unbeaten.

You daily achieve subtler levels of subordination with the three relative pronouns *that, which, who,* and with the conjunction *that. That, which,* and *who* connect thoughts so closely related as to seem almost equal, but actually each tucks a clause (subject-and-verb) into some larger idea:

> The car, *which* runs perfectly, is not worth selling.
> The car *that* runs perfectly is worth keeping.
> He thought *that* the car would run forever.
> He thought [*that* omitted but understood] the car would run forever.

But the subordinating conjunctions and adverbs (*although, if, because, since, until, where, when, as if, so that*) really put subordinates in their places. Look at *when* in this sentence of E. B. White's from *Charlotte's Web:*

> Next morning *when* the first light came into the sky and the sparrows stirred in the trees, *when* the cows rattled their chains and the rooster crowed and the early automobiles went whispering along the road, Wilbur awoke and looked for Charlotte.

Here the simple *when,* used only twice, has regimented five sub-ordinate clauses, all of equal rank, into their proper station below that of the main clause, "Wilbur awoke and looked for Charlotte." You can vary the ranking intricately and still keep it straight:

> *Although* some claim *that* time is an illusion, *because* we have no absolute chronometer, *although* the mind cannot effectively grasp time, *because* the mind itself is a kind of timeless presence almost oblivious to seconds and hours, *although* the time of our solar system may be only an instant in the universe at large, WE STILL CANNOT QUITE DENY *that* some progression of universal time is passing over us, *if* only we could measure it.

Complex sentences are at their best really simple sentences gloriously delayed and elaborated with subordinate thoughts. The following beautiful and elaborate sentence from the Book of Common Prayer is all built on the simple sentence "draw near":

> Ye who do truly and earnestly repent you of your sins, and are in love and charity with your neighbors, and intend to lead a new life, following the commandments of God, and walking from henceforth in his holy ways, draw near with faith, and take this holy sacrament to your comfort, and make your humble confession to Almighty God, devoutly kneeling.

Even a short sentence may be complex, attaining a remarkably varied suspense. Notice how the simple statement "I allowed myself" is skill-fully elaborated in this sentence by the late Wolcott Gibbs of the *New Yorker:*

> Twice in my life, for reasons that escape me now, though I'm sure they were discreditable, I allowed myself to be persuaded that I ought to take a hand in turning out a musical comedy.

Once you glimpse the complex choreography possible within the dimensions of the simple sentence, you are on your way to developing a prose capable of turns and graceful leaps, one with a kind of intellectual health that, no matter what the subject or mood, is always on its toes.

Try for still closer connections: modify.

Your subordinating *if*'s and *when*'s have really been modifying—that is, limiting—the things you have attached them to. But there is a smoother way. It is an adjectival sort of thing, a shoulder-to-shoulder operation, a neat trick with no need for shouting, a stone to a stone with no need for mortar. You simply put clauses and phrases up against a noun, instead of attaching them with a subordinator. This sort of modification includes the following constructions, all using the same close masonry: (1) appositives, (2) relatives understood, (3) adjectives-with-phrase, (4) participles, (5) absolutes.

Appositives. Those phrases about shoulders and tricks and stones, above, are all in apposition with *sort of thing*, and they are grammatically subordinate to it. The phrases are nevertheless nearly coordinate and interchangeable. They are compressions of a series of sentences ("It is an adjectival sort of thing," "It is a neat trick," and so forth) set side by side, "stone to stone." Mere contact does the work of the verb *is* and its subject *it*. English often does the same with subordinate clauses, omitting the *who is* or *which is* and putting the rest directly into apposition. "The William who is the Conqueror" becomes "William the Conqueror." "The Jack who is the heavy hitter" becomes "Jack the heavy hitter." These, incidentally, are called "restrictive" appositives, because they restrict to a particular designation the nouns they modify, setting this William and this Jack apart from all others (with no separating commas). Similarly, you can make nonrestrictive appositives from nonrestrictive clauses, clauses that simply add information (between commas). "Smith, who is a man to be reckoned with, . . ." becomes "Smith, a man to be reckoned with, ..." "Jones, who is our man in Liverpool, . . ." becomes "Jones, our man in Liverpool, ..." Restrictive or nonrestrictive, close contact makes your point. You glow with the pleasures of economy and fitness.

Relatives understood. You can often achieve the same economy, as I have already hinted, by omitting any kind of relative and its verb, thus gaining a compression both colloquial and classic:

A compression [that is] both colloquial and classic . . . .
The specimens [that] he had collected . . . .
The girl [whom] he [had] left behind . . . .

But be careful after verbs of feeling and seeing; omitting *that* may lead to confusion: "She felt his ears were too big." "He saw her nose was too small."

Adjectives-with-phrase. This construction is also appositive and adjectival. It is elegant, neat, and useful:

The law was passed, *thick with provisions and codicils, heavy with implications.*

There was the lake, *smooth in the early air.*

Participles.   Participles—verbs acting as adjectives—are extremely supple subordinators. Consider these three coordinate sentences:

He finally reached home. He discovered how tired he was. He went to bed without reading his mail.

Change the main verbs into present participles, and you can subordinate any two of the sentences to the other (so long as you still make sense), economizing on excess *He's*, balancing incidentals, and emphasizing the main point. You simply use the participles as adjectives to modify the subject *he:*

Finally *reaching* home, *discovering* how tired he was, he went to bed . . . .

The past participle has the same adjectival power:

Dead to the world, *wrapped* in sweet dreams, *untroubled* by bills, he slept till noon.

You will appreciate how like the adjective is the participle when you notice that *dead,* in the sentence above, is in fact an adjective, and that the participles operate exactly as it does.

Beware of participles that dangle, without clear reference to anything. They may trip you, as they have tripped others. The participle, with its adjectival urge, may grab the first noun that comes along, with shocking results:

Bowing to the crowd, the bull caught him unawares.
Observing quietly from the bank, the beavers committed several errors in judgment.
Squandering everything on beer, the money was never paid.
By bending low, the snipers could not see the retreating squad.
Tired and discouraged, half the lawn was still uncut.
What we need is a list of teachers broken down alphabetically.

Simply move the participle next to its intended noun or pronoun; you will have to supply this word if inadvertence or the passive voice has omitted it entirely. You may also save the day by changing a present participle to a past:

Observed quietly from the bank, the beavers . . . .
Squandered on beer, the money . . . .

Or you may move to ultimate sophistication by giving your participle a subject of its own within the phrase:

Every cent squandered on beer, the money was never paid.

Here is a sentence from Jane Austen's *Persuasion* that illustrates the adjectival and subordinating power of the participle—*delighted* twice modifying *She* and subordinating everything to the one basic four-word clause that begins the sentence:

> She always watched them as long as she could, delighted to fancy she understood what they might be talking of, as they walked along in happy independence, or equally delighted to see the Admiral's hearty shake of the hand when he encountered an old friend, and observe their eagerness of conversation when occasionally forming into a little knot of the navy, Mrs. Croft looking as intelligent and keen as any of the officers around her.

This sentence ends so gracefully because, with the phrase *Mrs. Croft looking*, it achieves the ultimate in participial perfection—the ablative absolute.

Absolutes. The absolute phrase has a great potential of polished economy. Many an absolute is simply a prepositional phrase with the preposition dropped:

> He ran up the stairs, [with] *a bouquet of roses under his arm*, and rang the bell.
> He walked slowly, [with] *his gun at the ready.*

But the ablative absolute is the supreme sophisticate of subordination. *Ablative* means "removed," and the ablative absolute is absolutely removed from grammatical connection with the main clause, modifying only by proximity. If you have suffered the rudiments of Latin, you will probably remember this construction as some kind of brusque condensation, something like "*The road completed,* Caesar moved his camp." But it survives in the best of circles. Somewhere E. B. White admits to feeling particularly good one morning, just having brought off an especially fine ablative absolute. The construction does have tone. And it is actually more common than you may suppose. A recent newspaper article stated that "the Prince has fled the country, *his hopes of a negotiated peace shattered.*" The *hopes shattered* pattern (noun plus participle) marks the ablative absolute. The idea might have been more conventionally subordinated: "since his hopes were shattered" or "with his hopes shattered." But the ablative absolute accomplishes the subordination with economy and style.

Take a regular subordinate clause: *"When* the road *was* completed." Cut the subordinator and the finite verb. You now have an ablative absolute, a phrase that stands absolutely alone, shorn of both its connective *when* and its full predication *was: "The road completed,* Caesar moved his camp." Basically a noun and a participle, or noun and adjective, it is a kind of grammatical shorthand, a telegram: *ROAD COMPLETED CAESAR MOVED*—most said in fewest words, speed with high compression. This is its appeal and its power.

> The cat stopped, its *back arched,* its *eyes frantic.*
> The whole economy, *God willing,* soon will return to normal.
> *All things considered,* the plan would work.
> The *dishes washed,* the *baby bathed* and *asleep,* the last *ash tray
>   emptied,* she could at last relax.

It is certainly a construction you should use with caution. It can sound exactly like a bad translation. But able writers come to it sooner or later, whether knowingly or through discovering for themselves the horsepower in a subordinate clause milled down to its absolute minimum of noun and participle, or noun and adjective, or even noun and noun. Hemingway uses it frequently. Here is one of the noun-noun variety at the end of a sentence about pistols in *To Have and Have Not:* ". . . their only *drawback the mess* they leave for relatives to clean up." And here are two of the noun-participle kind (*he playing* and *the death administered*), in a passage that will serve as a closing illustration of how a complex sentence can subordinate as many as 164 words to the 7 of its one main clause ("They will put up with mediocre work"):

> If the spectators know the matador is capable of executing a complete, consecutive series of passes with the muleta in which there will be valor, art, understanding and, above all, beauty and great emotion, THEY WILL PUT UP WITH MEDIOCRE WORK, cowardly work, disastrous work because they have the hope sooner or later of seeing the complete faena; the faena that takes a man out of himself and makes him feel immortal while it is proceeding, that gives him an ecstasy, that is, while momentary, as profound as any religious ecstasy; moving all the people in the ring together and increasing in emotional intensity as it proceeds, carrying the bullfighter with it, he playing on the crowd through the bull and being moved as it responds in a growing ecstasy of ordered, formal, passionate, increasing disregard for death that

leaves you, when it is over, and the death administered to the animal that has made it possible, as empty, as changed, and as sad as any major emotion will leave you.*

Parallel Construction

Use parallels wherever you can.

Hemingway's 171-word sentence could not have held together without parallel construction, the masonry of syntax. No complex sentence can sustain a very long arch without it. Actually, Hemingway's "that is" after "ecstasy" makes a false parallel, throwing his arch briefly out of line (he should have used "which is" or something like "an ecstasy as profound, though momentary, as any . . ."). You have also seen examples of parallel ranking in White's *when* sentence on page 37 and in the sentence that followed, dealing with time. The sentence about the cat and the one about the relaxing housewife on page 42 have shown you ablative absolutes laid parallel.

Parallel masonry can be very simple. Any word will seek its own kind, noun to noun, adjective to adjective, infinitive to infinitive. The simplest series of things automatically runs parallel:

shoes and ships and sealing wax
I came, I saw, I conquered
to be or not to be
a dull, dark, and soundless day
mediocre work, cowardly work, disastrous work

But they very easily run out of parallel too, and this you must learn to prevent. The last item especially may slip out of line, as in this series: "friendly, kind, unobtrusive, and *a bore*" (boring). Your paralleling articles and prepositions should govern a series as a whole, or should accompany *every* item:

a hat, a cane, a pair of gloves, and a mustache
a hat, cane, pair of gloves, and mustache
by land, by sea, or by air
by land, sea, or air

---

* *Death in the Afternoon* (New York: Charles Scribner's Sons, 1932), pp. 206–207. Copyright 1932 by Charles Scribner's Sons; renewal copyright © 1960 by Ernest Hemingway. Reprinted by permission of Charles Scribner's Sons.

Repeat your paralleling connectives.

When your series consists of phrases or of clauses, you should repeat the preposition or conjunction introducing them, to ensure clarity:

> *By* weeks of careful planning, *by* intelligence, *by* thorough training, and *by* a great deal of luck . . . .
>
> *Since* all things are not equal, *since* consequences cannot be foreseen, *since* we live but a moment . . . .
>
> He looked *for* clean fingernails and polished shoes, *for* an air of composure, and *for* a quick wit.

Watch the paralleling of pairs.

Pairs should be pairs, not odds and ends. Notice how the faulty pairs in these sentences have been corrected:

> She liked *the lawn and gardening* (tending the lawn and gardening).
>
> They were all *athletic or big men on campus* (athletes or big men on campus).
>
> He wanted *peace without being disgraced* (peace without dishonor).
>
> He liked *to play well and winning before a crowd* (to play well and to win; playing well and winning).
>
> She was *shy but an attractive girl* (shy but attractive).

Check your terms on both sides of your coordinating conjunctions (*and, but, or*) and see that they match:

> necessary
> Orientation week seems both worthwhile [adjective] and ~~a necessity~~ [noun].

> that
> He prayed that they would leave and ∧ the telephone would not ring.

Learn to use paralleling coordinators.

The first sentence above has used one of a number of useful (and tricky) parallel constructions: *Both/and; either/or; not only/ but also; not/but; first/second/third; as well as.* This last one is similar to *and*, a simple link between two equivalents, but it often causes trouble:

> A person should take care of his physical self [noun] *as well as* being [participle] able to read and write.

Again, the pair should be matched: "his physical self as well as his intellectual self," or "his physical self as well as his ability to read and write"—though this second is still slightly unbalanced, in rhetoric if not in grammar. The best cure would probably extend the underlying antithesis, the basic parallel:

> A person should take care of his physical self as well as his intellectual self, of his ability to survive as well as to read and write.

With the *either-or's* and the *not-only-but-also's*, you continue the principle of pairing. The *either* and the *not only* are merely signposts of what is coming: two equivalents linked by a coordinating conjunction (*or* or *but*). Beware of putting the signs in the wrong place—too soon for the turn:

(Either) he is an absolute piker or a fool.

(Neither) in time nor space . . . .

He (not only) likes the girl, but the family, too.

In these examples, the thought got ahead of itself, as in talk. Just make sure that the word following each of the two coordinators is of the same kind, preposition for preposition, article for article, adjective for adjective—for even with signs well placed, the parallel can skid:

> The students are not only organizing [present participle] social
>   discussing
> activities, but also are ~~interested~~ [passive construction] ~~in~~ political questions.

Put identical parts in parallel places; fill in the blanks with the same parts of speech: "not only _____, but also ____ _." You similarly parallel the words following numerical coordinators:

> However variously he expressed himself, he unquestionably thought, first, *that* everyone could get ahead; second, *that* workers generally were paid more than they earned; and, third, *that* laws enforcing a minimum wage were positively undemocratic.
> For a number of reasons he decided (1) that he did not like it, (2) that she would not like it, (3) that they would be better off without it.
> > [Note that the parentheses around the numbers operate just as any others, and need no additional punctuation.]

My objections are obvious: (1) it is unnecessary, (2) it costs too much, and (3) it won't work.

In parallels of this kind, *that* is usually the problem, since you may easily, and properly, omit it when there is only one clause and no confusion:

> . . . he unquestionably thought everyone could get ahead.

If second and third clauses occur, as your thought moves along, you may have to go back and put up the first signpost:

that

> . . . he unquestionably thought $\wedge$ everyone could get ahead, that workers . . . , and that laws . . . .

Enough of *that*. Remember simply that equivalent thoughts demand parallel constructions. Notice the clear and massive strategy in the following sentence from the concluding chapter of Freud's last book, *An Outline of Psychoanalysis*. Freud is summing up not only the previous discussion but the quintessence of his life's work. He is pulling everything together in a single sentence. Each of the parallel *which* clauses gathers up, in proper order, an entire chapter of his book (notice the parallel force in repeating *picture,* and the summarizing dash):

> The picture of an ego which mediates between the id and the external world, which takes over the instinctual demands of the former in order to bring them to satisfaction, which perceives things in the latter and uses them as memories, which, intent upon its self-preservation, is on guard against excessive claims from both directions, and which is governed in all its decisions by the injunctions of a modified pleasure principle—this picture actually applies to the ego only up to the end of the first period of childhood, till about the age of five.

Such precision is hard to match. This is what parallel thinking brings —balance and control and an eye for sentences that seem intellectual totalities, as if struck out all at once from the uncut rock. Francis Bacon also can seem like this (notice how he drops the verb after establishing his pattern):

> For a crowd is not company, and faces are but a gallery of pictures, and talk but a tinkling cymbal, where there is no love.

> Reading maketh a full man; conference a ready man; and writing an exact man.

And the balance can run from sentence to sentence through an entire passage, controlled not only by connectives repeated in parallel, but by whole phrases and sentences so repeated, as in this passage by Macaulay:

> To sum up the whole: we should say that the aim of the Platonic philosophy was to exalt man into a god. The aim of the Baconian philosophy was to provide man with what he requires while he continues to be man. The aim of the Platonic philosophy was to raise us far above vulgar wants. The aim of the Baconian philosophy was to supply our vulgar wants. The former aim was noble; but the latter was attainable.

The Long and Short of It

Your style will emerge once you can manage some length of sentence, some intricacy of subordination, some vigor of parallel, and some play of long against short, of amplitude against brevity. Try the very long sentence, and the very short. The best short sentences are meatiest:

> To be awake is to be alive.
> A stitch in time saves nine.
> The mass of men lead lives of quiet desperation.
> The more selfish the man, the more anguished the failure.

Experiment, too, with the fragment. The fragment is close to conversation. It is the laconic reply, the pointed afterthought, the quiet exclamation, the telling question. Try to cut and place it clearly (usually at beginnings and ends of paragraphs) so as not to lead your reader to expect a full sentence, or to suspect a poor writer:

> But no more.
> First, a look behind the scenes.
> Again: the man of reason.
> No, not really.
> Enough of that.

The conversational flow between long and short makes a passage move. Study the subordinations, the parallels, and the play of short and long in this elegant passage of Virginia Woolf's—after you have read it once for sheer enjoyment. She is writing of Lord Chesterfield's famous letters to Philip Stanhope, his illegitimate son:

> But while we amuse ourselves with this brilliant nobleman and his views on life we are aware, and the letters owe much of their fascina-

tion to this consciousness, of a dumb yet substantial figure on the farther side of the page. Philip Stanhope is always there. It is true that he says nothing, but we feel his presence in Dresden, in Berlin, in Paris, opening the letters and poring over them and looking dolefully at the thick packets which have been accumulating year after year since he was a child of seven. He had grown into a rather serious, rather stout, rather short young man. He had a taste for foreign politics. A little serious reading was rather to his liking. And by every post the letters came—urbane, polished, brilliant, imploring and commanding him to learn to dance, to learn to carve, to consider the management of his legs, and to seduce a lady of fashion. He did his best. He worked very hard in the school of the Graces, but their service was too exacting. He sat down half-way up the steep stairs which lead to the glittering hall with all the mirrors. He could not do it. He failed in the House of Commons; he subsided into some small post in Ratisbon; he died untimely. He left it to his widow to break the news which he had lacked the heart or the courage to tell his father—that he had been married all these years to a lady of low birth, who had borne him children.

The Earl took the blow like a gentleman. His letter to his daughter-in-law is a model of urbanity. He began the education of his grand-sons . . . .*

Those are some sentences to copy. We immediately feel the rhythmic play of periodic and loose, parallel and simple, long and short. Such orchestration takes years of practice, but you can always begin.

Exercises

1. Write three short sentences that invert normal order for emphasis: "That I like."

2. Write six simple sentences (make sure you have no subordinate clauses), two complicating the subject, two the verb, and two the object.

3. Write six compound sentences, two with *and,* two with *but,* two with *or (nor).* Try to get as grand a feeling of consequence as possible: "Empires fall, and the saints come marching in."

4. Write three compound sentences using conjunctive adverbs, on the

---

* *The Second Common Reader* (New York: Harcourt, Brace, 1932), p. 81. Copyright 1932 by Harcourt, Brace; renewed © 1960 by Leonard Woolf. Reprinted by permission of Harcourt Brace Jovanovich, Inc., and The Hogarth Press, Ltd.

pattern: "_____; therefore, _____ "—punctuated carefully with semi-colon and comma.

5. List all the subordinators you can think of (*since, if, before,* etc.).

6. Write five sequences of three simple sentences on the pattern: "He finally reached home. He was tired. He went to bed." Then, changing verbs to participles, subordinate two of the sentences to the remaining one in each sequence.

7. To appreciate participial subordination, rewrite each of the following as a series of simple coordinate sentences, changing the participles into finite verbs and the principal adjectives into predicate adjectives ("They danced. They swayed . . . . Some were intense."):

> They danced, swaying in dim light, dreaming happily, some laughing, some intense, some even embarrassed and awkward, wishing but failing to join the dream completely.
>
> He was every inch a soldier, clipped, tailored, polished, as if straight from a musical comedy.
>
> His train already late, his money stolen, his hat gone, his plans upset from start to finish, he hoped desperately that he still had time.
>
> Complicated, misleading, inadequate, and motivated by special interests, the bill deserved defeat.

8. Review the discussion of parallel coordinators on pages 44–46. Then write a sentence for each of the following sets of coordinators. Try different parts of speech, but keep your parallels true by filling the blanks in any one sentence with the same parts of speech.

> both _____ and _____
> either _____ or _____
> not only _____ but also _____
> (1) _____ , (2) _____ , (3) _____
> _____ as well as _____

9. Write six sentences with dangling participles, with a remedy for each.

10. Write six sentences with ablative absolutes, three using present participles, three using past.

11. Now, write a hundred-word sentence *with only one independent clause,* and with everything else subordinated.

12. Adjust or clarify the parallels in the following (taken from freshmen papers):

> These men are not only cheating themselves, but also are banded

together into crime syndicates which help to lower the character of the entire nation.

He stated two ways in which man could hope to continue survival. (1) World citizenship, or (2) destroying most of the inventions that man is uncertain of and go back to where we can understand ourselves and progress.

In this way not only the teacher needs to be concerned with the poorest student, but every class member helped.

A student follows not only a special course of training, but among his studies and social activities finds a liberal education.

When they go to church, it is only because they have to go and not of their own desire.

This is not only the case with the young voters of the United States but also of the adult ones.

. . . an education which will not only embarrass her but also is dangerous to a self-governing people.

Certain things are not actually taught in the classroom. They are learning how to get along with others, to depend on oneself, and managing one's own affairs.

Every time I sit down and attempt to read one of those interesting essays, or else studying German . . . .

Knowing Greek and Roman antiquity is not just learning to speak their language but also their culture.

I think fraternities are sociable as well as the dormitories.

13. In the following famous sentence of Bacon's, straighten the faulty parallels and fill out all the phrasing implied by them:

Histories make men wise; poets witty; the mathematics subtle; natural philosophy deep; moral grave; logic and rhetoric able to contend.

6
Correcting
Bad Sentences

Now let us contemplate evil—or at least the innocently awful, the bad habits that waste our words, fog our thoughts, and wreck our delivery. Our thoughts are naturally roundabout, our phrases naturally secondhand. Our satisfaction in merely getting something down on paper naturally blinds us to our errors and ineptitudes. Writing is devilish. It hypnotizes us into believing we have said what we meant, when our words actually say something else: "Every seat in the house was filled to capacity." Good sentences therefore come from constant practice in correcting the bad.

Count your words.

The general sin is wordiness. We put down the first thought that comes, we miss the best order, and we then need lengths of *is*'s, *of*'s, *by*'s, and *which*'s—words virtually meaningless in themselves— to wire our meaningful words together again. Look for the two or three words that carry your meaning; then see if you can't rearrange them to speak for themselves, cutting out all the little useless wirings:

> This is the young man who was elected to be president by the class.
> [The class elected this young man president. *7 words for 14*]

See if you can't promote a noun into a verb, and cut overlaps in meaning:

> Last week, the gold stampede in Europe reached near panic proportions. [Europe's gold rush almost *stampeded* last week. *7 words for 11*]

By converting the noun *stampede* into the verb *stampeded*, you can cut the overlapping "near panic proportions": stampedes *are* panics.

The ungrammatical and misleading *near* (for *nearly* or *almost*) is usually a symptom of wordiness.

The basic cure is to count the words in any suspected sentence—and to make each word count. If you can rephrase to save even one word, your sentence will be clearer. And seek the active verb: *John* ʜɪᴛ *Joe.*

Avoid the passive voice.

The passive voice drones like nothing under the sun, leaving active English dead to the world:

> **It was voted that there would be a drive for the cleaning up of the people's park. [*passive voice—17 words*]**
> **We voted a drive to clean up the people's park. [*active voice—10 words*]**

The passive voice puts the cart before the horse: the object of the action first, then the harnessing verb, running backwards, then the driver forgotten, and the whole contraption at a standstill. The passive voice is *not* the past tense (*was, were, voted*); it is *not* the third person (*he, they, it*). It is simply "passive" action, the normal action backwards: object-verb-subject (with the true subject usually forgotten) instead of subject-verb-object—*Joe was hit by John* instead of *John hit Joe.*

The passive voice liquidates and buries the active individual, along with most of the awful truth. Our massed, scientific, and bureaucratic society is so addicted to it that you must constantly alert yourself against its drowsy, impersonal pomp. The simple English sentence is active; it *moves* from subject through verb to object: "Smith laid the cornerstone on April 1." But because we must sound important, because the impersonal institution must be bigger than Smith, the historian writes "The cornerstone was laid on April 1," and Smith vanishes from the earth. The doer and the writer both—all traces of individuality, all human interest—disappear behind the elongated passive verb: *was laid* instead of *laid.* The impersonal bureau emits a passive smokescreen, and the student sees no one at all to help him:

> **It has been decided that your proposal for independent study is not sufficiently in line with the prescribed qualifications as outlined by the college in the catalog.**

Committees always write this way, and the effect on academic writing, as the professor goes from committee to desk to classroom, is astounding. "It was moved that a meeting would be held," the secretary writes, to avoid pinning the rap on anybody. So writes the professor, so writes the student.

I reluctantly admit that the passive voice has certain uses. It can, in a string of active sentences, give mere variety, although phrasal and clausal variations are better. It can also vary the emphasis, and the interest, by inverting normal order. *Joe was hit by John* throws selective light on Joe, by inverting regular consequences and distinguishing him from all other unfortunates, and it gives John a certain dubious distinction too. The passive voice can, indeed, eliminate the doer with meaningful effect. *Joe was hit.* ("I was sunk." "It was done.")

In fact, your meaning sometimes demands the passive voice; the agent may be better under cover—insignificant, or unknown, or mysterious. The active "Shrapnel hit him" seems to belie the uncanny impersonality of "He was hit by shrapnel." The broad forces of history similarly demand the passive: "The West was opened in 1848." Moreover, you may sometimes need the passive voice to place your true subject, the hero of the piece, where you can modify him conveniently: *Joe was hit by John, who, in spite of all* . . . . And sometimes it simply is more convenient: "This subject-verb-object sentence can be infinitely contorted." You can, of course, find a number of passive constructions in this book, which preaches against them, because they can also space out a thought that comes too fast and thick. In trying to describe periodic sentences, for instance (p. 33), I changed "until all interconnections lock in the final word" (active) to ". . . are locked by the final word" (passive). The *lock* seemed too tight, especially with *in*, and the locking seemed contrary to the way buildings are built. Yes, the passive has its uses.

But it is wordy. It puts useless words in a sentence. Its dullness derives as much from its extra wordage as from its impersonality. *Joe was hit by John* says no more than *John hit Joe*, but takes 66 percent more words! The passive's inevitable *was* and *by* do nothing but connect; worse, all the *was*'s and *by*'s and *has been*'s actually get in the way of the words carrying the meaning, like underbrush slowing you down and hiding what you want to see.

The best way to prune is with the active voice, cutting the passive and its fungus as you go. Notice the effect on the following typical, and actual, samples:

Public concern *has* also *been given* a tremendous impetus *by* the

findings of the Hoover Commission on the federal government, and "little Hoover" commissions to survey the organizational structure and functions of many state governments *have been established.* [In the federal government, the findings of the Hoover Commission *have* also greatly stimulated public concern, and many states *have established* "little Hoover" commissions to survey their governments. *28 words for 38*]

The algal mats *are made up of* the interwoven filaments of several genera. [The interwoven filaments of several genera *make up* the algal mats. *11 words for 13*]

Many of the remedies *would* probably *be shown to be* faith cures. [Many of the remedies *are* probably faith cures. *8 words for 12*]

Anxiety and emotional conflict *are lessened* when latency sets in. The total personality is *oriented* in a repressive, inhibitory fashion so as to maintain the barriers, and what Freud has called "psychic dams," against psychosexual impulses. [When latency sets in, anxiety and emotional conflict *subside.* The personality *inhibits* itself, maintaining its barriers—Freud's "psychic dams"—against psychosexual impulses. *22 words for 36*]

The passive voice, simply in its wordiness, is always a bit unclear even on the surface; but, if it eliminates the real subject of the verb, as it usually does, it is intrinsically unclear as well. "This passage has been selected because . . . ," the student will write, and the reader cannot tell who did the selecting. Does he mean that he, the writer, has picked it, or does he describe some process of natural or popular selection? We surmise he means himself, of course; but why doesn't he say so, and save a word, and avoid confusion? "I selected this passage because . . . ."

The passive can also keep you from finding your true meaning:

The different tones in Joyce's stories *are achieved by* the frustrations of an author ill at ease in Dublin.

That sounds good—until you test it actively: "Frustrations achieve different tones." How? You must mean that *Joyce* achieved the tones, or that the frustrations put in the sour notes as they also drove Joyce to the happier reaches of imagination. Whichever way, the active voice brings cause and effect to the surface, where you can discover their true alignment.*

---

* I am grateful to George L. Grant, San Jose State College, for this valuable point, and the example.

Your alignment may also slip from active to passive, losing your subject in transit:

> As he *entered* the room, voices *could be heard*. [As he *entered* the room, he *could hear* voices.]
> After they *laid out* the pattern, electric shears *were used* to cut around it. [After they *laid out* the pattern, they *cut* around it with electric shears.]
> The first problem *is* political, but *there are* questions of economics involved in the second problem. [The first problem *is* purely political; the second, partly economic.]

Sometimes the subject will slip even in active sentences: "A *film* can improve upon a book, but *they* [it] usually *do* [does] not." But root out the passive voice, and most misalignments disappear.

Check the symptoms.

Begin by suspecting every *is:* it may mean a passive. Our language must use some form of *is* so frequently in stating that things *are* and in forming its compound verbs (*is falling, were playing*) that you should drop as many *is*'s and *was*'s as possible, simply to avoid monotony. But when they are—as they often are—signs of the passive voice, you can also avoid rigor mortis by replacing your *is*'s with active verbs, along with their true subjects, the real doers of the action.

To be, itself, frequently ought not to be:

> He seems [to be] upset about something.
> She considered him [to be] perfect.
> This appears [to be] difficult.

Similarly, in restrictive clauses (p. 70), many an improper *which,* and many a *that, who,* and *whom* as well, may depart, and good riddance:

> The rule [which] the committee favors . . . .
> I think [that] he should go.
> The man [whom] I respect . . . .

Above all, keep your sentences awake by not putting them into those favorite stretchers of the passivists, *There is . . . which, It is . . . that,* and the like:

> Moreover, [there is] one segment of the population [which] never seeks employment.
> [There are] many women [who] never marry.

[There] is nothing wrong with it.
[It is] his last book [that] shows his genius best.
[It is] this [that] is important.

The bracketed words can disappear without a ripple. Furthermore, *It is* frequently misleads your readers by seeming to mean something specific (*beer*, in the following example):

> Several members voted for beer. *It is* hard to get *it* through some people's heads that minors can't buy it. [Some people never learn that minors can't buy it.]

Cut every *it* not referring to something. Next to activating your passives, and cutting the passivistic *there is*'s and *it is*'s, perhaps nothing so improves your prose as to go through it systematically deleting every *to be*, every *which, that, who,* and *whom* not needed for utter clarity or for spacing out a thought. All of your sentences will feel better.

Beware the of-and-which disease.

The passive sentence also breaks out in a rash of *of*'s and *which*'s, and even the active sentence may suffer. Diagnosis: something like sleeping sickness. *With*'s, *in*'s, *to*'s, and *by*'s also inflamed. Surgery imperative. Here is a typical, and actual, case:

> Many biological journals, especially those *which* regularly publish new scientific names, now state *in* each issue the exact date *of* publication *of* the preceding issue. *In* dealing *with* journals *which* do not follow this practice, or *with* volumes *which* are issued individually, the biologist often needs *to* resort *to* indexes . . . *in order to* determine the actual date *of* publication *of* a particular name.

Note *of publication of* twice over, and the three *which*'s. The passage is a sleeping beauty. The longer you look at it the more useless little attendants you see. Note the inevitable passive voice (*which are issued*) in spite of the author's active efforts. The *of*'s accompany extra nouns, *publication* repeating *publish*, for instance. Remedy: (1) eliminate *of*'s and their nouns, (2) change *which* clauses into participles, (3) change nouns into verbs. You can cut more than a third of this passage without touching the sense (using 42 words instead of 63):

> Many biological journals, especially those regularly *publishing* new scientific names, now give in each issue the date of the one preceding. With journals not *following* this practice, and with some books, the biologist must turn to indexes . . . *to date* a particular name.

I repeat: you can cut most *which*'s, one way or another, with no loss of blood. Participles can modify their antecedents directly, since they are verbal adjectives, without an intervening *which:* "a car *which was* going south" is "a car going south"; "a train *which is* moving" is "a moving train." Similarly with the adjective itself: "a song *which was* popular last year" is "a song popular last year"; "a person *who is* attractive" is "an attractive person." Beware of this whole crowd: *who are, that was, which are.*

If you need a relative clause, remember *that. Which* has almost completely displaced it in labored writing. *That* is still best for restrictive clauses, those necessary to definition: "A house that faces north is cool" (a participle would save a word: "A house facing north is cool"). *That* is tolerable; *which* is downright oppressive. *Which* should signal the nonrestrictive clause (the afterthought): "The house, which faces north, is a good buy." Here you need *which.* Even restrictive clauses must turn to *which* when complicated parallels arise. "He preaches the brotherhood of man *that* everyone affirms" elaborates like this: "He preaches the brotherhood of man *which* everyone affirms, *which* all the great philosophies support, but *for which* few can make any immediate concession." Nevertheless, if you need relatives, a *that* will often ease your sentences and save you from the *which*'s.

Verbs and their derivatives, especially present participles and gerunds, can also help to cure a string of *of*'s. Alfred North Whitehead, usually of clear mind, once produced this linked sausage: "Education is the acquisition *of* the art *of* the utilization *of* knowledge." Anything to get around the three *of*'s and the three heavy nouns would have been better: "Education instills the art of using knowledge," or "Education teaches us to use knowledge well." Find an active verb for *is the acquisition of,* and shift *the utilization of* into some verbal form: the gerund *using,* or the infinitive *to use.* Shun the *-tion*'s! Simply change your surplus *tion*'s and *of*'s—along with your *which* phrases—into verbs, or verbals (*to use, learning*). You will save words, and activate your sentences.

Beware the use of.

In fact, both *use* as a noun and *use* as a verb are dangerously wordy words. Since "using" is one of our most basic concepts, other words in your sentence will already contain it:

He uses rationalization. [He rationalizes.]
He uses the device of foreshadowing. [He foreshadows.]

Through [the use of] logic, he persuades.
His [use of] dialogue is effective.

The utilization of and *utilize* are only horrendous extremes of the same pestilence, to be stamped out completely.

Break the noun habit.

Passive writing adores the noun, modifying nouns with nouns in pairs, and even in denser clusters—which then become official jargon. Break up these logjams, let the language flow, make one noun of the pair an adjective:

> *Teacher militancy* is not as marked in Pittsburgh. [*Teachers* are not so *militant* in Pittsburgh. *7 words for 8*]

Or convert one noun to a verb:

> *Teacher power* is less in evidence in Pittsburgh. [*Teachers demand* less in Pittsburgh. *5 words for 8*]

Of course, nouns have long served English as adjectives, as in "*rail*road," "*railroad* station," "*court*house," and "*noun* habit." But modern prose has aggravated the tendency beyond belief; and we get such monstrosities as *child sex education course,* whole strings of nothing but nouns. Professors of education, sociology, and psychology are the worst noun stringers, the hardest for you not to copy if you take their courses. But we have all caught the habit. The nouns *level* and *quality* have produced a rash of redundancies. A meeting of "high officials" has now unfortunately become a meeting of "high-*level* officials." The "finest cloth" these days is always "finest *quality* cloth." Drop those redundant nouns and you will make a good start, and will sound surprisingly original. You can drop many an excess noun:

WORDY	DIRECT
advance notice	notice
long in size	long
puzzling in nature	puzzling
of an indefinite nature	indefinite
of a peculiar kind	peculiar
in order to	to
by means of	by
in relation to	with
in connection with	with
1974-model car	1974 car

Wherever possible, find the equivalent adjective:

of great importance	important
highest significance level	highest significant level
government spending	governmental spending
reaction fixation	reactional fixation
sex education	sexual education
teaching excellence	excellent teaching
encourage teaching quality	encourage good teaching

Or change the noun to its related participle:

advance placement	advanced placement
charter bus	chartered bus
uniform police	uniformed police
poison arrow	poisoned arrow

Or make the noun possessive:

reader interest	reader's interest
factory worker wage	factory worker's wage
veterans insurance	veterans' insurance

Or try a cautious *of:*

WRONG	RIGHT
color lipstick	color of lipstick
teaching science	science of pedagogy
production quality	quality of production
high quality program	program of high quality
significance level	level of significance
a Marxist-type program	a Marxist program *or*
	a Marxist type of program

Of all our misused nouns, *type* has become peculiarly pestilential and trite. Advertisers talk of *detergent-type cleansers* instead of *detergents;* educators, of *apprentice-type situations* instead of *apprenticeships;* newspapermen, of *fascist-type organizations* instead of *fascistic organizations.* Don't copy your seniors; write boldly. We have become a nation of hairsplitters, afraid to say *Czechoslovakia's Russian tanks* for fear the reader will think they really belong to Russia. So the reporter writes *Russian-type tanks*, making an unnecessary distinction, and cluttering the page with one more *type-type* expression. We have forgotten that making the individual stand for the type is the simplest and oldest of metaphors: "Give us this day our daily bread." A twentieth-century man might have written "bread-type food."

The simple active sentence transmits the message by putting each word unmistakably in its place, a noun as a noun, an adjective as an adjective, with the verb—no stationary *is*—really carrying the mail. Recently, after a flood, a newspaper produced this apparently succinct and dramatic sentence: "Dead animals cause water pollution." (The word *cause*, incidentally, indicates wasted words.) That noun *water* as an adjective throws the meaning off and takes 25 percent more words than the essential active message: "Dead animals pollute water." As you read your way into the sentence, it seems to say "Dead animals cause water" (which is true enough), and then you must readjust your thoughts to accommodate *pollution*. The simplest change is from *water pollution* (noun-noun) to *polluted water* (adjective-noun), clarifying each word's function. But the supreme solution is to make *pollute* the verb it is, and the sentence a simply active message in which no word misspeaks itself. Here are the possibilities, in a scale from most active and clearest to most passive and wordiest, which may serve to chart your troubles if you get tangled in causes and nouns:

Dead animals pollute water.
Dead animals cause polluted water.
Dead animals cause water pollution.
Dead animals are a factor in causing the pollution of water.
Dead animals are a serious factor in causing the water pollution situation.
Dead farm-type animals are a danger factor in causing the post-flood clearance and water pollution situation.

So the message should now be clear. Write simple active sentences, outmaneuvering all passive eddies, all shallow *is*'s, *of*'s, *which*'s and *that*'s, all overlappings, all rocky clusters of nouns: they take you off your course, delay your delivery, and wreck many a straight and gallant thought.

Exercises

1. Write three sentences in the passive voice, and change each to its active equivalent.

2. Pick three obese and passive sentences from your textbooks (including this one, if the author has slipped). Change them to clean, active sentences, indicating the number of words saved in each.

3. Find in your textbooks a passage suffering from the *of*-and-*which* disease, *the-use-of* contagion, and the noun habit ("which shows the effect of age and intelligence level upon the use of the reflexes and the emergence of child behavior difficulties") and rewrite it in clear English.

4. Following the examples on pages 53–54, recast these sentences in the active voice, clearing out all passive constructions, saving as many words as you can, and indicating the number saved:

> One exercise approved by the committee is given to the class by the instructor. [Starting with "The instructor," you can say this in 11 words for 14.]
>
> The particular topic chosen by the instructor for study in his section of English 2 must be approved by the Steering Committee. [Start with "The Steering Committee," and don't forget the economy of an apostrophe-*s*. I managed 13 words for 22.]
>
> Avoidance of such blunders should not be considered a virtue for which the student is to be commended, any more than he would be praised for not wiping his hands on the tablecloth or polishing his shoes with the guest towels. [Begin "We should not"; try *avoiding* for *avoidance*. I dropped *virtue* as redundant and scored 34 for 41.]
>
> The first respect in which too much variation seems to exist is in the care with which writing assignments are made. ["First, care in assigning"—8 for 21.]
>
> The remaining variations that will be mentioned are concerned not with the assignment of papers but with the marking and grading of them. ["Finally, I shall mention"—11 for 23.]
>
> The difference between restrictives and nonrestrictives can also be better approached through a study of the different contours that mark the utterance of the two kinds of element than through confusing attempts to differentiate the two by meaning. ["One can differentiate restrictives"—I managed 13 for 38.]

5. Here are seven more to prune, especially of *that*'s, *which*'s, *who*'s, and *there is . . . which*'s. Take your pick, or try them all (my figures again are merely guides; other solutions are equally good):

> *There is* a certain tendency to defend one's own position *which* will cause the opponent's argument to be ignored. [14 for 19]
>
> *It is* the other requirements *that* present obstacles, some *of which* may prove insurmountable in the teaching of certain subjects. [13 for 20]
>
> In the sort of literature-centered course being discussed here, *there is* usually a general understanding *that* themes will be based on the various literary works *that* are studied, the theory

being *that* both the instruction in literature and *that* in writing will be made more effective by this interrelationship. [18 for 50]

The person *whom* he met was an expert *who was* able to teach the fundamentals quickly. [11 for 16]

They will take a pride *which is* wholly justifiable in being able to command a prose style *that is* lucid and supple. [13 for 22]

The work *which is* reported *in this* study *is* an investigation *of* language *within* the social context *of* the community *in which it is spoken. It is* a study *of* a linguistic structure *which is* unusually complex, but no more than the social structure *of* the city *in which it* functions. [I tried two versions, as I chased out the *which's*; 29 for 52, and 22 for 52.]

Methods *which are* unique to the historian *are illustrated* throughout the volume *in order to* show how history *is written* and how historians work. The historian's approach to his subject, *which* leads to the asking of provocative questions and to a new understanding of complex events, situations, and personalities *is probed.* The manner *in which* the historian reduces masses of chaotic fact—and occasional fancy—to reliable meaning, and the way *in which* he formulates explanations and tests them *is examined and clarified* for the student. *It is its* emphasis on historical method *which* distinguishes this book from other source readings in western civilization. The problems *which are examined* concern *themselves with* subjects *which are dealt with by* most courses in western civilization. [82 for 123]

7
Punctuation

Punctuation gives the silent page some of the breath of life. It marks the pauses and emphases with which a speaker points his meaning. Loose punctuators forget what every good writer knows: that even silent reading produces an articulate murmur in our heads, that language springs from the breathing human voice, that the beauty and meaning of language depend on what the written word makes us *hear*, on the sentence's tuning of emphasis and pause. Commas and semicolons and periods do what they can to transcribe our meaningful pauses to the printed page.

The Period: Sentences and Fragments

Learn what a sentence is.

Having used sentences all our lives, we all think we know what one is. But commas still appear where periods should be, and the reader blunders ahead when he should have stopped. Think of a *sentence* as a subject completed in its verb and tacked home with a period. We rarely mistake a *phrase* for a sentence, since, having no verb, it cries for completion. But a *clause*, which does have subject and verb, is indeed a complete sentence—unless it looks to the main sentence for fulfillment:

After the ball [phrase], **the sweepers come.**
After the ball *is over* [clause], **the sweepers come.**

Your sentence is complete if the first part clearly looks ahead toward the period, and if the end clearly looks back toward its beginning. If you find the first part of your sentence looking back, or looking ahead in vain, you have no sentence; you have a fragment that should be hooked, with a comma, where it belongs:

He dropped his teeth. *Which had cost two hundred dollars.*

A good example is Hawthorne. *A writer who can dramatize abstract moral theories.*

Cleopatra is the stronger. *Trying to create Antony in her own Egyptian image.*

The accidental fragment is almost invariably found *after* its governing sentence.

But try an occasional rhetorical fragment.

Nothing so firmly demonstrates your command over the sentence as a judicious fragment, as I have already suggested (p. 47). Make it stand alone, and no mistake. Fragments are safest and most effective, with all their transitional force, at the head of a paragraph. Such fragments are especially dramatic, economical, and close to speech.

First, a word to the wise.
Another point.
Of course.
Not at all.
Expert within limits, that is.

Notice that all these fragments—condensations, afterthoughts, answers, quiet exclamations—usually omit some hypothetical form of *is*, with its subject:

First, [here is] a word to the wise.
Of course [it is *or* he did].
[It is] not at all [so].

This kind of dramatic fragment, in other words, is talking about existences, about what *is*, letting the words assert their own being— exactly the kind of streamlining the Latin writers liked, and still swift and racy. But be careful.

The Comma

Learn the rules.

You need only four. Use a comma:

I. Before the coordinator—*and, but, for, or, nor, yet, still*—when joining independent clauses.
II. Between all terms in a series, *including the last two.*

III. To set off parenthetical openers and afterthoughts.

IV. Before and after parenthetical insertions (use a *pair* of commas).

Rule I. Put a comma before conjunctions such as and, but, *and* for *when joining independent clauses.*

You will be told that you may omit the comma when your two clauses are short: "He hunted and she fished." You certainly can get away with it, and in the best of publications. But it is really the first tiny slip toward utter abandon. Your clauses will grow longer. You will begin to touch in a comma only now and then, still leaving the main gap between clauses unplugged. You will omit commas before *but* and *for* and really throw your reader off. Nothing is wrong with "He hunted, and she fished." With the comma, in fact, it shows the slight pause you make when you say it. Stick to the rule, and you can't go wrong. And you will greatly improve your sense of style.

Think of the "comma-*and*" as a unit equivalent to the period and the semicolon. All three join independent clauses, but with different emphases:

   .   He was tired. He went home.

   ;   He was tired; he went home.

 , and He was tired, and he went home.

If you can only think of the , **and** or the , **but** as a unit, perfectly equivalent to the . and the ; as a buffer between independent clauses, you will have mastered the basic problem in punctuation, the cause of most trouble.

What you need is a firm rule to follow. You may find exceptions— or what seem exceptions until you see the underlying reasons, since good punctuation expresses meaning. Look again at White's *when* sentence (p. 37):

> Next morning when the first light came into the sky and the sparrows stirred in the trees, when the cows rattled their chains and the rooster crowed and the early automobiles went whispering along the road, Wilbur awoke . . . .

White omits several commas before *and,* but the reason is dazzlingly clear. He is regimenting short coordinate clauses under one subordinator, *when.* A comma after *sky,* for instance, would block the *when* from the *sparrows* and throw the clauses out of rank. For reasons of rank, he also omits the "introductory" comma after *Next morning.* A comma here, since only two other commas control the whole long sentence, would have thrown *Next morning* into sudden prominence, into unjustified equality with the long *when* elements.

Your punctuation, or lack of it, signals your meaning as it comes in, word by word. The **, and** tells your reader that a whole new predication is coming; just-plain-**and** tells him to expect only a smaller unit:

He hunted the hills and . . . .

brings an entirely different expectation from

He hunted the hills, and . . . .

In the first, you expect something like *dales,* something parallel to *hills.* In the second, you expect another subject and predicate: "and he found . . . ," or "and they were . . . ."

Omitting the comma between independent clauses joined by *and* really makes a false parallel, and the silence of print often encourages the error. When you *say* "hills and dales," you do not pause. When you *say* ". . . hills, and he found . . . ," you do pause. English invariably expresses this difference in meaning by pausing or not. Modern linguists, who call this pause a "double-bar juncture," have reminded us that commas signify meaning.

The same may be seen with *but, or,* and *yet:*

She was naughty but nice.
She was naughty, but that is not our business.

Wear your jacket or coat.
Wear your jacket, or you will catch cold.

It was strong yet sweet.
It was strong, yet it was not unpleasant.

Of course, you may use a comma in *all* the examples above if your sense demands it. The contrast set by *but, or,* and *yet* often urges a comma, whether or not full predication follows: "It was strong, yet sweet." Notice that the commas always signal where you would pause in speaking.

The meaningful pause also urges an occasional comma in compound predicates, usually not separated by a comma:

He granted the usual permission and walked away.
He granted the usual permission, and walked away.

Both are correct. In the first sentence, however, the granting and walking are perfectly routine, and the temper unruffled. In the second, some kind of emotion has forced a pause, and a comma, after *per-mission*. Similarly, meaning itself may demand a comma between the two verbs:

He turned and dropped the ball.
He turned, and dropped the ball.

In the first sentence, he turned the ball; in the second, himself. Your *, and* in compound predicates suggests some touch of drama, some meaningful distinction or afterthought.

You need a comma before *for* and *still* even more urgently. Without a comma, their conjunctive meaning changes; they assume their ordinary roles, *for* as a preposition, *still* as an adjective or adverb:

She liked him still . . . . [that is, either *yet* or *quiet!*]
She liked him, still she could not marry him.
She liked him for his money.
She liked him, for a good man is hard to find.

An observation: *for* is the weakest of all the coordinators. Almost a subordinator, it is perilously close to *because*. *For* can seem moronic if cause and effect are fairly obvious: "She liked him, for he was kind." Either make a point of the cause by full subordination—"She liked him *because* he was kind"—or flatter the reader with a semicolon: "She liked him; he was kind." *For* is effective only when the cause is somewhat hard to find: "Blessed are the meek, for they shall inherit the earth."

Rule II. Put commas between all terms in a series, including the last two:

words, phrases, or clauses in a series
to hunt, to fish, and to hike
He went home, he went upstairs, and he could remember nothing.
He liked oysters, soup, roast beef, wine, and women.

The linguists' recordings will show a pause between the last two items of a series as well as between any two: not *wine-and-women,* but *wine, and women.* The good punctuator would drop the last comma only if he meant *wine and women* as a unit equivalent to *oysters.* Since the last element will always have some climactic or anticlimactic effect, solemn or humorous, don't blur it into the one preceding. Keep *wine and women* separate.

By carefully separating all elements in a series, you keep alive a final distinction long ago lost in the daily press, the distinction Mrs. Woolf makes (see p. 48): "urbane, polished, brilliant, imploring and commanding him . . . ." *Imploring and commanding* is syntactically equal to each one of the other modifiers in the series. If Mrs. Woolf customarily omitted the last comma, as she does not, she could not have reached for that double apposition. The muscle would have been dead. These other examples of double apposition will give you an idea of its effectiveness:

> They cut out his idea, root and branch.
> He lost all his holdings, houses and lands.
> He loved to tramp the woods, to fish and to hunt.

A comma makes a great deal of difference, of sense and distinction.

But adjectives in series, as distinct from nouns in series, change the game a bit. Notice the difference between the following two strings of adjectives:

> a good, unexpected, natural rhyme
> a good old battered hat

With adjectives in series only your sense can guide you. If each seems to modify the noun directly, as in the first example above, use commas. If each seems to modify the total accumulation of adjectives and noun, as with *good* and *old* in the second phrase, do not use commas. Say your phrases aloud, and put your commas in the pauses that distinguish your meaning. Finally, a special case. Dramatic intensity sometimes allows you to join clauses with commas, instead of the usual periods or semicolons:

> She sighed, she cried, she almost died.
> I couldn't do it, I tried, I let them all get away.
> It passed, it triumphed, it was a good bill.
> I came, I saw, I conquered.

The rhetorical intensity of this construction—the Greeks called it *asyndeton*—is obvious. The language is breathless, or grandly emphatic. As Aristotle once said, it is a person trying to say many things at once. The subjects repeat themselves, the verbs overlap, the idea accumulates a climax. By some psychological magic, the clauses of this construction usually come in three's. The comma is its sign. But unless you have a stylistic reason for such a flurry of clauses, go back to the normal "comma-*and*," semicolon, or period, or you will have a comma splice: a comma where a period or semicolon should be.

Rule III. Set off parenthetical openers and afterthoughts with a comma.

Again, note the preliminary pause that expresses your meaning:

Besides, she hated it.
Inside, everything was snug.
Stunned, he opened the telegram.
Thoroughly disgruntled, he left.
Green with envy, she smiled weakly.
For several reasons, they stayed home.
Being of stout heart, he dieted.
A good man at poker, he still failed at bridge.
Although several looked bored, he kept on talking.
Because it never gets cold, they wear few clothes.
If it is not too much trouble, punctuate accurately.

First observation: A comma often makes all the difference:

However she tried, she could not do it.
However, she tried.
However she tried. [??]

Solution: *NEVER* begin with *However* unless you mean "In whatever way." Begin with *But,* and bury your *however's* (as conjunctive adverbs) within the sentence between commas: "She tried, however, a little longer."

With afterthoughts, the rule still holds: ordinarily you should set them off with a comma. But close sequences of cause and effect (even in openers) often make the comma optional with *for, because,* and *if,* and occasionally with others:

They stayed home for several reasons.
For several reasons they stayed home.
Everything was snug inside.
They wear few clothes because it never gets cold.
Punctuate accurately if you can.

Emphasis makes the difference. A comma would have damaged none of them (when in doubt, follow the rule); it would merely have changed their rhetoric.

Rule IV. Enclose parenthetical insertions with a pair of commas.

Here you are cutting the sentence in two and inserting something necessary. But if you do not tie off both ends, your sentence will die on the table:

When he packs his bag, however he goes.
The car, an ancient Packard is still running.
April 10, 1990 is agreeable as a date for final payment.
That handsome man in the ascot tie, is the groom.
John Jones, Jr. is wrong.

You do not mean that 1990 is agreeable, or that Junior is wrong. All parenthetical insertions need a *pair* of commas:

The case, *nevertheless*, was closed.
She will see, *if she has any sense at all*, that he is right.

The same rule applies, of course, to *nonrestrictive* remarks, phrases, and clauses—all elements that are simply additive, explanatory, and hence parenthetical:

John, *my friend*, will do what he can.
Andy, *his project sunk, his hopes shattered*, was speechless.
The taxes, *which are reasonable*, will be paid.
That man, *who knows*, is not talking.

Think of *nonrestrictive* as "nonessential" to your meaning, hence set off by commas. Think of *restrictive* as essential and "restricting" your meaning, hence not set off at all (use *which* for nonrestrictives, *that* for restrictives; see p. 57):

The taxes that are reasonable will be paid.
Southpaws who are superstitious will not pitch on Friday nights.
The man who knows is not talking.

Commas are often optional. The difference between a restrictive and a nonrestrictive meaning may be very slight. For example, you may take our recent bridegroom either way (but not halfway):

That handsome man, in the ascot tie, is the groom. [nonrestrictive]
That handsome man in the ascot tie is the groom. [restrictive]

Your meaning will dictate your choice. But use *pairs* of commas or none at all. Never separate subject and verb, or verb and object, with just one comma.

Some finer points. One comma of a pair enclosing an inserted remark may coincide with, and, in a sense, overlie, a comma "already there":

In each box, a bottle was broken.
In each box, however, a bottle was broken.

The team lost, and the school was sick.
The team lost, in spite of all, and the school was sick.

> The program will work, but the cost is high.
> The program will work, of course, but the cost is high.

Between the coordinate clauses, however, a semicolon would be clearer:

> The team lost, in spite of all; and the school was sick.

Beware: *however* between commas cannot substitute for **, but**, as in the perfectly good sentence "He wore a hat, *but* it looked terrible." You would be using a comma where a full stop (period or semicolon) should be.

WRONG:

> He wore a hat, however, it looked terrible.

RIGHT (*notice the two meanings*):

> He wore a hat; however, it looked terrible.
> He wore a hat, however; it looked terrible.

But a simple **, but** avoids both the ambiguity of the floating *however* and the ponderosity of anchoring it with a semicolon, fore and aft: "He wore a hat, but it looked terrible."

Another point. *But* may absorb the first comma of a pair enclosing an introductory remark (although it need not do so):

> At any rate, he went.
> But, at any rate, he went.
> But at any rate, he went.
> But [,] if we want another party, we had better clean up.
> The party was a success, but [,] if we want another one, we had better clean up.

And of course you should put the comma *inside* ALL quotation marks:

> "He is a nut," she said.
> She called him a "nut," and walked away.

Semicolon and Colon

Use the semicolon only where you could also use a period, unless desperate.

The semicolon is neither a weak colon nor a strong comma. It is a kind of tight period, a separator of contrasts. *Never* use it as a colon: its effect is exactly opposite. A colon, as in the preceding sentence, is a green light; a semicolon, as in this sentence, is a stop sign.

Of course, you may occasionally need to unscramble a long line of phrases and clauses:

> You should see that the thought is full, the words well cleaned, the
> points adjusted; and then your sentence will be ready to go.
>> [Note that the period rule would still guide you here:
>> ". . . adjusted. And then . . . ."]
> Composition is hard because we often must discover our ideas by
> writing them out, clarifying them on paper; because we must find
> a clear and reasonable order for ideas the mind presents simul-
> taneously; and because we must find, by trial and error, exactly the
> right words to convey our ideas and our feelings about them.

But the semicolon is better when it pulls related sentences together:

> She liked him; he was good to her; he had money in the bank.

And better still when it pivots a contrast:

> Work when you work; play when you play.
> The semicolon is a stop sign; the colon, a green light.

Notice that the semicolon (like the colon) goes *outside* quotation marks:

> This was no "stitch in time"; it was complete reconstruction.

The colon is the green light, perfect for introducing quotations or itemized series (see p. 149), or for speeding the thought through intersections:

> The point is precisely this: no one can win.
> Pierpont lived for only one thing: money.

Parenthesis and Dash

The dash says aloud what the parenthesis whispers. Both enclose interruptions too extravagant for a pair of commas to hold. The dash is the more useful—since whispering tends to annoy—and will remain useful only if not overused. A well-cultivated dash will give you the ultimate in urbane control. It can serve as a conversational colon. It can set off a concluding phrase—for emphasis. It can bring long introductory matters to focus, as in Freud's sentence on page 46. It can insert a full sentence—a clause is really an incorporated sentence —directly next to a key word. With a dash, you can insert—with a kind of shout!—an occasional exclamation. You can even insert—and who would blame you?—an occasional question. The dash affords a structural complexity with all the tone and alacrity of talk. But don't forget the force of a whisper:

> Many philosophers have despaired (somewhat unphilosophically) of ultimate certainties.
> Delay had doubled the costs (a stitch in time!), so the plans were shelved.

When one of a pair of dashes falls where a comma would be, it absorbs the comma:

> If one wanted to go, he certainly could.
> If one wanted to go—whether he was invited or not—he certainly could.

Not so with the semicolon:

> He wanted to go—whether he was invited or not; she had more sense.

To indicate the dash, type two hyphens (--) flush against the words they separate—not one hyphen between two spaces, nor a hyphen looking exactly like a hyphen.

Put commas and periods *outside* a parenthetical group of words (like this one). (But if you make an entire sentence parenthetical, put the period inside.)

Brackets

Brackets indicate your own words inserted or substituted within a quotation from someone else: "Byron had already suggested that [they] had killed John Keats." You have substituted "they" for "the gentleman of the *Quarterly Review*" to suit your own context; you do the same when you interpolate a word of explanation:

> "Byron had already suggested that the gentlemen of the *Quarterly Review* [especially Croker] had killed John Keats."

Do not use parentheses: they mark the enclosed words as part of the original quotation. Don't claim innocence because your typewriter lacks brackets. Just leave spaces and draw them in later, or type slant lines and tip them with pencil or with the score key:

$$\lceil\; . \; . \; . \rceil$$

Quotation Marks and Italics

Put quotation marks around quotations that "run directly into your text" (like this), but *not* around long quotations set off from the text and indented (and single-spaced in typing). Periods and commas go *inside* quotation marks; semicolons and colons go *outside*.

> This was no "stitch in time"; it was complete reconstruction.
> This was another "thorn in the side."
> He thought that "seeing is believing," until today.
> In Greece, it was "know thyself"; in America, it is "know thy neighbor."
> He left after "Hail to the Chief": he could do nothing more.

Although logic seems to demand the period or comma outside the quotation marks, convention has put them inside for the sake of appearance, even when the sentence ends in a single quoted word or letter:

> Clara Bow was said to have "It."
> He uses the first-personal "I."

If you have seen the periods and commas outside, you were reading a British book or a freshman paper.

If you quote a phrase already containing quotation marks, reduce the original double marks (") to single ones ('):

ORIGINAL	YOUR QUOTATION
Hamlet's "are you honest?" is easily explained.	"Hamlet's 'are you honest?' is easily explained."

Notice what happens when the quotation within your quotation falls at the end:

ORIGINAL	YOUR QUOTATION
The Japanese call albatross "aho dori."	Jones reports, "The Japanese call albatross 'aho dori.'"

An indirect quotation omits quotation marks, unless already within the original:

> He writes that Hamlet's "are you honest?" is easily explained.
> He says that psychotherapy is reclamation, like draining the Zuyder Zee.

When quoting only part of a sentence, adjust your own sentence to include it grammatically:

ORIGINAL	YOUR SENTENCE
My hands are clean as a hound's tooth.	Mr. Carr mixed both his issues and his figures of speech, declaring his hands as "clean as a hound's tooth."

Use quotation marks for titles *within* books and magazines, and for statues and paintings; use italics for books, plays, movies, long poems, ships, trains, and airplanes:

His story "Too Much Gas" appeared in the *Atlantic Monthly.*
He wrote *The Decline and Fall of the Roman Empire.*
The *Spirit of St. Louis* is more famous than the *Titanic.*

Italicize foreign words (*casus belli, idée fixe*) and words as words, or for emphasis (see almost any page in this book). You underscore a word to italicize it, preferably breaking the underscore after each word in italicized phrases, as also in titles.

Ellipsis

(1) Use three spaced periods . . . (the ellipsis mark) when you omit something from a quotation. Do *not* use them in your own text in place of a dash, or in mere insouciance. (2) If you omit the end of a sentence, add the period . . . ✓(3) If your omission falls after a completed sentence, add the ellipsis mark to the period already there✓. . . . I have put a check over the periods. Notice the difference in spacing. Note that each placement of the ellipsis means something different.

Here is an uncut passage, followed by a shortened version that shows in succession the three kinds of ellipsis, with the third appearing in two variations:

> To learn a language, learn as thoroughly as possible a few everyday sentences. This will educate your ear for all future pronunciations. It will give you a fundamental grasp of structure. Some of the details of grammar will begin to appear. It will give you confidence. If you go abroad, you can buy a newspaper and find your way back to the hotel.

(1)
To learn a language, learn . . . a few everyday sentences. This will
(2)
educate your ear . . . . It will give you a fundamental grasp of

(3)   (3)

structure. . . . It will give you confidence. . . . you can buy a newspaper and find your way back to the hotel.

The three spaced dots of the ellipsis may fall on either side of other
punctuation, to indicate exactly where you have omitted something
from the text you are quoting:

In many instances of human crisis, . . . words are superfluous.
We have the bombs . . . ; it looks as if they have the troops.

Apostrophe

Add *'s* to form the singular possessive, even with words already ending
in *s* (*dog's life, Yeats's poems, Marx's ideas, Charles's crown, Leavis's
error*). A few plurals also form the possessive by adding *'s* (*children's
hour, men's room, women's pool, mice's holiday, sheep's bellwether*).
But most plurals take the apostrophe after the *s* (*witches' sabbath, the
Browns' house, citizens' rights*).

Some people merely add the apostrophe after words ending in *s:
boss' daughter, Williams' edict, Sis' plans.* But we say *boss's daughter*
("bossuz daughter") and *Sis's plans,* and we should write, and say,
Williams's edict, Dickens's novels, and *Adams's horse* to distinguish
Williams from William, Dickens from Dicken, and Adams from Adam.

The apostrophe can help to clarify clusters of nouns: *Alistair Jones
Combo* is *Alistair Jones's Combo;* the *country church rummage sale*
is the *country church's rummage sale; student protest* is *students'
protest.* Distinguish your modifiers, and keep your possessions.

Use the apostrophe to indicate omissions: *the Spirit of '76, the Class
of '02, can't, won't, don't.* Finally, use the apostrophe when adding a
grammatical ending to a number, letter, sign, or abbreviation: *1920's;*
his *3's* look like *8's; p's* and *q's;* he got four *A's;* too many *of's* and
and's; she *X'd* each box; *K.O.'d* in the first round.

Hyphen

Hyphenate two or more words serving together as an adjective: "a
fish-and-chips man," "the *not-too-distant* future." Unhyphenated words
acquire hyphens when moved to an adjectival position:

She teaches in high school.
She is a high-school teacher.

Hyphenate prefixes to proper names (*anti-Semitism, un-American*) and suffixes to single capital letters (*T-shirt, I-beam, X-ray*). Hyphenate *ex-champions* and *self-reliances*. Hyphenate to avoid double *i*'s and triple consonants: *anti-intellectual, bell-like*. Hyphenate two-word numbers: *twenty-one, three-fourths*. Use the "suspensive" hyphen for hyphenated words in series:

We have ten-, twenty-five-, and fifty-pound sizes.

Exercises

1. Write three fragments that are unmistakable accidents, crying out for attachment to some governing sentence. Then write three complete sentences with these fragments properly attached.

2. Write three groups of three or four sentences, each group containing a rhetorical fragment that cannot be mistaken for a mistake.

3. Write six pairs of sentences, using the six conjunctions *and, but, for, or, yet, still,* on the pattern:

He hunted the hills and . . . .
He hunted the hills, and . . . .

4. Write three sentences with concluding double appositives which might look like parts of a simple series but which are not: "He loved to camp, to hunt and to fish."

5. Write three or four asyndetic sentences (see p. 68), each with three clauses.

6. Master *however* by writing three or four groups of three sentences on the following pattern:

However she tried, she could not do it.
She tried, however, a very long time.
She tried; however, she could not do it.

7. Write three or four pairs of sentences to practice enclosing parenthetical insertions within a pair of commas:

April 10 is fine.
April 10, 1990, is fine.

The taxes will be paid.
The taxes, which are reasonable, will be paid.

8. Do the same with dashes and with parentheses.

9. Write three pairs of sentences showing the difference between non-restrictive and restrictive clauses, on the pattern:

The taxes, which are reasonable, will be paid.
The taxes that are reasonable will be paid.

10. Write three compound sentences, using a semicolon between two contrasting independent clauses.

8
Words

Here is the word. Sesquipedalian or short, magniloquent or low, Latin or Anglo-Saxon, Celtic, Danish, French, Spanish, Indian, Hindustani, Dutch, Italian, Portuguese, Chinese, Hebrew, Turkish, Greek—a million words at our disposal, if we are disposed to use them. Although no language is richer than English, our expository vocabularies average probably fewer than eight thousand words. We could all increase our active vocabularies; we all have a way to go to possess our inheritance.

Vocabulary

If you can increase your hoard, you increase your chances of finding the right word, *le mot juste,* when you need it. Read as widely as you can, and look words up the second or third time you meet them. I once knew a man who swore he learned three new words a day from his reading by using each at least once in conversation. I didn't ask him about *polyphiloprogenitive* or *antidisestablishmentarianism.* It depends a little on the crowd. But the idea is sound. The bigger the vocabulary the more various the ideas one can get across with it—the more the shades and intensities of meaning.

The big vocabulary also needs the little word. The vocabularian often strands himself on a Roman cloud and forgets the Anglo-Saxon ground—the common ground between him and his audience. So do not forget the little things, the *stuff, lint, get, twig, snap, go, mud, coax.* Hundreds of small words not in immediate vogue can refresh your vocabulary. The Norse and Anglo-Saxon adjectives ending in -*y* (*muggy, scrawny, drowsy*), for instance, rarely appear in sober print. The minute the beginner tries to sound dignified, in comes a misty layer of words a few feet off the ground and nowhere near heaven, the same two dozen or so, most of them verbs. One or two will do no harm, but any accumulation is fatal—words like *depart* instead of *go:*

accompany—go with
appeared—looked *or* seemed
arrive—come
attempt—try
become—get
cause—make
cease—stop
complete—finish
continue—keep on
delve—dig
discover—find
locate—find

place—put
possess—have
prepare—get ready
questioned—asked
receive—get
relate—tell
remain—stay
remove—take off
retire—go to bed
return—go back
secure—get
transform—turn

I add one treasured noun: *manner—way.* The question, as always, is one of meaning. *Manner* is something with a flourish; *way* is the usual way. But the beginner makes no distinctions, losing the normal *way,* and meaning, in a false flourish of *manners.* Similarly, "She *placed* her cigarettes on the table" is usually not what the writer means. *Delve* is something that happens only when students begin to meditate. *Get* and *got* may be too colloquial for regular writing, but a discreet one or two can limber many a stiff sentence. Therefore, fit the elegant Latin to the commonplace Anglo-Saxon. But shun the frayed gentility of *secure* and *place* and *remain,* whose shades of meaning you can find in your dictionary.

Abraham Lincoln read the dictionary from cover to cover, and you really can browse it with pleasure, looking at the pictures and finding out about aardvarks and axolotls, jerboas and jerkins. You can amaze yourself at the number of things *set* can mean. Best of all, you can look at a word's derivation and get a quick sense of our linguistic history, of families of words and ideas, of how some meanings have changed and some have persisted through centuries and across continents. *Mid,* for instance, is still what it has been for the last five thousand years, persisting in most of the Indo-European languages all the way from Old Norse to Sanskrit, and giving English a whole family of words from *middle* to *intermezzo.* Acquaintance with a family can make you feel at home. You can know and use a *ramp,* or a *rampage,* or a lion *rampant* familiarly, once you see the Old French for *climb* in all three. You can cut your meaning close to the old root, as in "He was *enduring* and *hard* as nails," where the Latin *durus* ("hard") has suggested its Anglo-Saxon synonym and given you a phrase your readers will like, though most of them won't know why.

Through the centuries, English has added Latin derivatives along-side the Anglo-Saxon words already there, keeping the old with the new: after the Anglo-Saxon *deor* (now *deer*) came the *beast* and then the *brute,* both from Latin through French, and the *animal* straight from Rome. Although we use more Anglo-Saxon in assembling our sentences (*to, by, with, though, is*), well over half our total vocabulary comes one way or another from Latin. The things of this world tend to be Anglo-Saxon (*man, house, stone, wind, rain*); the abstract qualities, Latin and French (*value, duty, contemplation*).

Our big words are Latin and Greek. Your reading acquaints you with them; your dictionary will show you their prefixes and roots. Learn the common prefixes and roots (see Exercises, this chapter), and you can handle all kinds of foreigners at first encounter: *con-cession* (going along with), *ex-clude* (lock out), *pre-fer* (carry before), *sub-version* (turning under), *trans-late* (carry across), *claustro-phobia* (dread of being locked in), *hydro-phobia* (dread of water), *ailuro-philia* (love of cats), *megalo-cephalic* (big-headed), *micro-meter* (little measurer). You can even, for fun, coin a word to suit the occasion: *megalopede* (big-footed). You can remember that *intramural* means "within the (college) walls," and that *intermural sports,* which shows the frequent mispronunciation and misspelling, would mean some-thing like "wall battling wall," a physical absurdity.

Besides a good dictionary, you should own a good edition of Roget's *Thesaurus,* the treasury of synonyms ("together-names"), in which you can find the word you couldn't think of, and all the shades of good and bad you want, from *pants* through *trousers* to *galligaskins. The Diction-ary of Synonyms* also helps you to the word and meaning you want—to be checked again in your dictionary.

Abstract and Concrete

Every good stylist has perceived, in one way or another, the distinc-tion between abstract and concrete words. Tangible things—things we can touch—are "concrete"; their qualities, along with all our emo-tional, intellectual, and spiritual states, are "abstract." The rule for a good style is to be as concrete as you can, to illustrate tangibly your general propositions, to use *shoes* and *ships* and *sealing wax* instead of *commercial products.* But this requires constant effort: our minds so crave abstraction that we can hardly pin them down to specifics.

Abstraction, a "drawing out from," is the very nature of thought. Thought moves from concrete to abstract. In fact, *all* words are abstractions. *Stick* is a generalization of all sticks, the crooked and the straight, the long and the short, the peeled and the shaggy. No word fits its object like a glove, because words are not things: words represent our *ideas* of things. They are the means by which we class eggs and tents and trees so that we can handle them as ideas—not as actual things but as *kinds* of things. A man can hold an egg in his hand, but he cannot think about it, or talk about it, unless he has some larger idea with which his mind, too, can grasp it, some idea like *thing*, or *throwing thing*, or *egg*—which classes this one white ellipsoid with all the eggs he has known, from ostrich to hummingbird, with the *idea* of egg. One word for each item would be useless; it would be no idea at all, since ideas represent not items, but *classes* of items.

In fact, abstract words can attain real power, as the writer heightens attention to their meanings. In his dedication at Gettysburg, Lincoln thus concentrates on the idea of *dedication* six times in his famous ten sentences, each time with a slightly different force, squeezing the abstract idea for its specific juice: "We have come to *dedicate* . . . . It is rather for us to be here *dedicated* . . . ." Indeed, abstractions can operate as specifics: "As a knight, Richard the Lion-hearted was *a triumph;* as a king, he was *a disaster.*"

So before we disparage abstraction, we should acknowledge its rhetorical power; and we should understand that it is an essential distillation, a primary and natural and continual mental process. We cannot do without it. We could not make four of two and two. So we make abstractions of abstractions to handle bigger and bigger groups of ideas. *Egg* becomes *food,* and *food* becomes *nourishment.* We also classify all the psychic and physical qualities we can recognize: *candor, truth, anger, beauty, negligence, temperament.* But because our thoughts drift upward, we need always to look for the word that will bring them nearer earth, that will make our abstractions seem visible and tangible, that will make them graspable. We have to pull them down within reach of our reader's own busily abstracting headpiece.

We must pin our abstractions down with constant comparisons to the concrete eggs from which they sprang. I might have written that sentence—as I found myself starting to do: "Abstractions should be actualized by a process of constant comparisons with the concrete objects which they represent." But note what I have done to pull this down within reach. First, I have used *we;* that is, you and I, real people. I have cut the inhuman passive voice to put us in the act. Then I have changed *actualize* to *pin down,* a visible action that, being commonplace and proverbial, makes us feel at home among the abstractions. I have replaced the abstract *by a process of* with its simpler abstract equivalent, *with.* More important, I have made *eggs* stand for all objects—and note how easily our abstracters take this in. Furthermore, I have punned on *concrete,* making it, for a fleeting instant, into cement. How? By choosing *egg,* something that could really be made out of concrete, instead of *stick* (which I had first put there): a concrete stick is not much as a physical possibility. Finally, I have gone on to use *egg* also as a real egg by having the abstract ideas spring from it. Later, I almost changed *sprang* to *hatched,* but decided that this was too vivid. It would make the concrete egg too nearly real, and the picture of broken cement with fluffy abstractions peeping forth would have gotten in the way of the idea—that is, the disembodied abstract concept—I was trying to convey.

But the writer's ultimate skill perhaps lies in making a single concrete object represent its whole abstract class. I have paired each abstraction below with a good concrete translation:

Friendliness is the salesman's best asset.
A *smile* is the salesman's best asset.

A *proper protein diet* might have saved John Keats.
A good *steak* might have saved John Keats.

To *understand* the world by *observing all its geological details* . . . .
To *see* the world in a *grain of sand* . . . .

Metaphor

As you have probably noticed, I have been using metaphors—the most useful way of making our abstractions concrete. The word is Greek for "transfer" (*meta* equals *trans* equals *across; phor* equals *fer* equals *ferry*). The idea is that of representing something as if it were something else, objects as if all of them were eggs, abstractions as if they were chickens that are also vaguely like flowers springing, thought as if it were rising steam. Metaphors illustrate, in a word, our general ideas. I might have written at length about how an idea is like an egg. I did, in fact, follow each declaration with an example, and I illustrated the point with a man holding an egg. But the metaphor makes the comparison at a stroke. I used our common word *grasp* for "understanding," comparing the mind to something with hands, *transferring* the physical picture of the clutching hand to the invisible mental act.

Almost all our words are metaphors, usually with the physical picture faded. *Transfer* itself pictures a physical portage. When the company *transfers* its men, it is sending them about the country as if by piggyback, or raft, or whatever. But mercifully the physical facts have faded—*transfer* has become a "dead metaphor"—and we can use the word in comfortable abstraction. Now, precisely because we are constantly abstracting, constantly letting the picture fade, you can use metaphor to great advantage—or disastrously, if your eyes aren't sharp. With metaphors you avoid the nonpictorial quality of most of our writing; you make your writing both vivid and unique. As Aristotle said, the metaphor is clear, agreeable, and strange; like a solved riddle, it is the most delightful of teachers.

Metaphor works at about four levels, each with a different clarity and force (and, as you will see, we must here distinguish between the general idea of "metaphor" as the whole process of transfer, and that specific thing called "a metaphor"):

Simile:	She was *like* a horse.
	She stopped *as* a horse stops.
	She stopped *as if* she were a horse.
Metaphor:	She was a horse.
Implied metaphor:	She snorted and tossed her mane.
Dead metaphor:	She bridled.

The simile is the most obvious of the metaphors, and hence would seem elementary. But it has powers of its own, particularly in its *as if* variation, where the writer seems to be trying urgently to express the inexpressible, comparing his subject to several different possibilities, no one wholly adequate. In *The Sound and the Fury*, Faulkner thus describes two jaybirds (my italics):

> [they] whirled up on the blast *like gaudy scraps of cloth or paper* and lodged in the mulberries, . . . screaming into the wind that ripped their harsh cries onward and away *like scraps of paper or of cloth* in turn.

The simile has a high poetic energy. D. H. Lawrence uses it frequently, as in the following paragraph (my italics) from *The Plumed Serpent*:

> The lake was quite black, *like a great pit.* The wind suddenly blew

with violence, with a strange ripping sound in the mango trees, *as if some membrane in the air were being ripped.*

The plain metaphor makes the comparison in one imaginative leap. It is shorthand for "as if she were a horse"; it pretends, by exaggeration (*hyperbole*), that she *is* a horse. We move instinctively to this kind of exaggerated comparison as we try to convey our impressions with all their emotional impact. "He was a maniac at Frisbee," we might say, "a dynamo, a computer." The metaphor is probably our most common figure of speech: *the pigs, the swine, a plum, a gem, a phantom of delight, a shot in the arm.* It may be humorous or bitter; it may be simply and aptly visual: "The road was a ribbon of silver."

The implied metaphor is even more widely useful. It operates most often among the verbs, as in *snorted* and *tossed,* the horsey verbs suggesting "horse." Most ideas can suggest analogues of physical processes or natural history. Give your television system *tentacles reaching into every home,* and you have compared TV to an octopus, with all its lethal and wiry suggestions. You can have your school spirit *fall below zero.* You can even pun on the physical Latin components in our abstract words, turning them back into their original suggestions of physical acts, as in "The *enterprise* grabbed everything" (some beast or army is rushing in), for *enterprise* means in Latin something like "to rush in and grab." Too subtle? No, the contrast between *enterprise* and *grabbed* will please anyone, and the few who see it all will be delighted.

Enterprise is really a dead metaphor, and resuscitation is the metaphorist's finest skill. It comes from liking words, and paying attention to what they say. The punster makes the writer, if he can restrain himself. Simply add onto the dead metaphor enough implied metaphors to get the circulation going again. *She bridled, snorting and tossing her mane. She bridled* means, by itself, as we have abstracted it, nothing more than "reacted disdainfully." By bringing the metaphor back to life, we keep the general meaning but also restore the physical picture of a horse lifting its head and arching its neck against the bridle. This is exhilarating. We recognize *bridle* concretely and truly for the first time. We know the word, and we know the woman. We have an image of her, a posture vaguely suggestive of a horse.

Perhaps the best dead metaphors to revive are those in proverbial clichés. See what Thoreau does (in his journal) with *spur of the moment:*

**I feel the spur of the moment thrust deep into my side. The present is
an inexorable rider.**

Or again, when in *Walden* he speaks of wanting "to improve the nick
of time, and notch it on my stick too," and of not being *thrown off the
track* "by every nutshell and mosquito's wing that falls on the rails."
In each case, he takes the proverbial phrase literally and physically,
adding an attribute or two to bring the old metaphor back alive.

You can go too far, of course. The metaphors can be too thick and
vivid, and the obvious pun brings a howl of protest. Jane Austen
disliked metaphors, as Mary Lascelles notes in *Jane Austen and Her
Art,* and reserved them for her hollow characters. I myself have advised
scholars not to use them because they are so often overworked and
so often tangled in physical impossibilities. "The violent population
explosion has paved the way for new intellectual growth" looks pretty
good—until you realize that explosions do not pave, and that new
vegetation does not grow up through pavement. The metaphor, then,
is your most potent device. It makes your thought concrete, and your
writing vivid. It tells in an instant how your subject looks to you. But
it is dangerous. It should be quiet, almost unnoticed, with all details
agreeing and all absolutely consistent with the natural universe.

Allusion

Allusions also illustrate your general idea by referring it to something
else, making it take your reader as Grant took Richmond, making you
the Mickey Mantle of the essay, or the Mickey Mouse. Allusions depend
on common knowledge. Like the metaphor, they illustrate the remote
with the familiar—a familiar place, or event, or personage. "He looked
. . . like a Japanese Humphrey Bogart," writes William Bitner of
French author Albert Camus, and we instantly see a face like the one
we know so well. (A glance at Camus's picture confirms how accurate
this unusual allusion is.) Perhaps the most effective allusions depend
on a knowledge of literature. When Thoreau writes that "the winter of
man's discontent was thawing as well as the earth," we get a secret
pleasure from recognizing this as an allusive borrowing from the opening lines of Shakespeare's *Richard III:* "Now is the winter of our dis-
content/Made glorious summer by this sun of York." Thoreau flatters
us by assuming we are as well read as he. We do not need to catch the
allusion to enjoy his point, but if we catch it, we do feel a sudden

fellowship of knowledge with him. We now see the full metaphorical force, Thoreau's and Shakespeare's both, heightened as it is by our remembrance of Richard Crookback's twisted discontent, an allusive illustration of all our pitiful resentments now thawing with the coming of spring.

Diction

"What we need is a mixed diction," said Aristotle, and his point remains true twenty-three centuries and several languages later. The aim of style, he says, is to be clear but distinguished. For clarity, we need common, current words; but used alone, these are commonplace, and as ephemeral as everyday talk. For distinction, we need words not heard every minute, unusual words, strange words, foreign words, metaphors; but used alone, these become gibberish. What we need is a diction that marries the popular with the dignified, the clear current with the sedgy margins of language and thought.

Not too low, not too high; not too simple, not too hard—an easy breadth of idea and vocabulary. English is peculiarly well endowed for this Aristotelian mixture. The long abstract Latin words and the short concrete Anglo-Saxon ones give you all the range you need. For most of your ideas you can find Latin and Anglo-Saxon partners. In fact, for many ideas you can find a whole spectrum of synonyms from Latin through French to Anglo-Saxon, from general to specific: from *intrepidity* to *fortitude* to *valor* to *courage* to *bravery* to *pluck* to *guts.* You can choose the high word for high effect, or you can get tough with Anglo-Saxon specifics. But you do not want all Anglo-Saxon, and you must especially guard against sobriety's luring you into all Latin. Tune your diction agreeably between the two extremes.

Indeed, the two extremes generate incomparable zip when tumbled side by side, as in *incomparable zip, inconsequential snip, megalocephalic creep,* and the like. Rhythm and surprise conspire to set up the huge adjective first, then to add the small noun, like a monumental kick. Here is a passage from Edward Dahlberg's *Can These Bones Live,* which I opened completely at random to see how the large fell with the small (my italics):

Christ walks on a *visionary sea;* Myshkin . . . has his ecstatic premonition of infinity when he has an *epileptic fit.* We know the inward size of an artist by his *dimensional thirsts . . . .*

This mixing of large Latin and small Anglo-Saxon, as John Crowe Ransom has noted, is what gives Shakespeare much of his power:

> **This my hand will rather**
> **The multitudinous seas incarnadine,**
> **Making the green one red.**

The short Anglo-Saxon *seas* works sharply between two magnificent Latin words, as do the three short Anglo-Saxons that bring the big passage to rest, contrasting the Anglo-Saxon *red* with its big Latin synonym, *incarnadine.* William Faulkner, who soaked himself in Shakespeare, gets much the same power from the same mixture. He is describing a very old Negro woman in *The Sound and the Fury* (the title itself comes from Shakespeare's *Macbeth,* the source of the *multitudinous seas* passage). She has been fat, but now she is wrinkled and completely shrunken except for her stomach:

> **. . . a paunch almost dropsical, as though muscle and tissue had been**
> **courage or fortitude which the days or the years had consumed until**
> **only the indomitable skeleton was left rising like a ruin or a landmark**
> **above the somnolent and impervious guts . . . .**

The impact of that short, ugly Anglo-Saxon word, with its slang metaphorical pun, is almost unbearably moving. And the impact would be nothing, the effect slurring, without the grand Latin preparation. "What we need is a mixed diction."

Beware of wordiness.

Verbosity is a disease. Symptoms: severe inflation of the language, difficulty in following the point, extreme drowsiness. Cause: too much Latin and the passive voice (see pp. 52–56). Cure: making words count, and administering moderate doses of Anglo-Saxon. In speaking of sentences earlier, I commended elaboration. But I also recommended deletion. A fully worded sentence, each word in place and pulling its weight, is a joy to see. But a sentence full of words is not. Words should count, I say again. And the best way to make them count is to count the words in each dubious case. Any shorter version will be clearer. I once counted the words, sentence by sentence, in a thirty-page manuscript rejected as "too loose." In some sentences, I cut no more than one or two words. I rephrased many, but I think I cut no entire sentence. In fact, I added a considerable paragraph; and I still had five pages fewer, and a better essay.

Sentences can be too short and dense, of course. Many thoughts need explanation and an example or two. Many need the airing of *and*'s and *of*'s. Many simply need some loosening of phrase. In fact, colloquial phrasing, which is as clear and unnoticed as a clean window, is usually longer than its formal equivalent: *something to eat* as compared to *dinner*. By all counts, *dinner* should be better. It is shorter. It is more precise. Yet *something to eat* has social delicacy (at least as I am imagining the party). "Shall we have something to eat?" is more friendly than the more economical "Shall we have dinner?" We don't want to push our friends around with precise and economical suggestions. We want them at their ease, with the choices slightly vague. Consequently, when we write *what we are after* for *object* and *how it is done* for *method*, we give our all-too-chilly prose some social warmth. These colloquial phrases take more words, but they are not wordy if they pull with the rest of the sentence.

It all comes down to redundancy, the clutter of useless words and tangential ideas—"the accumulation of words that add nothing to the sense and cloud up what clarity there is," as Aristotle says. What we write should be easy to read. Too many distinctions, too many nouns, and too much Latin can be pea soup:

> **Reading is a processing skill of symbolic reasoning sustained by the interfacilitation of an intricate hierarchy of substrata factors that have been mobilized as a psychological working system and pressed into service in accordance with the purpose of the reader.**

This comes from an educator, with the wrong kind of education. He is saying:

> **Reading is a process of symbolic reasoning aided by an intricate network of ideas and motives.**

Our educator has fallen into jargon, that official language of every trade, unintelligible to everyone else. The English professor has his *plot structure* when he means *plot*, his *structure* when he means *idea*. The psychologist has his *action reactions*. Avoid all jargon—by breaking the noun habit (*plot structure*) and by insisting that your words say what they mean.

Try *not* to define your terms. If you do, you are probably either evading the toil of finding the right word, or defining the obvious:

> **Let us agree to use the word signal as an abbreviation for the phrase "the simplest kind of sign." (This agrees fairly well with the customary meaning of the word "signal.")**

Now, really! That came from a renowned semanticist, a student of the meanings of words. A word's customary meaning *is* its meaning, and uncustomary meanings come only from careful punning. Don't underestimate your readers, as this semanticist did.

The definer of words is usually a bad writer. Our semanticist continues, trying to get his signals straight and grinding out about three parts sawdust to every one of meat. In the following excerpt, I have bracketed his sawdust. Read the sentence first as it was written; then read it again, omitting the bracketed words:

> **The moral of such examples is that all intelligent criticism [of any instance] of language [in use] must begin with understanding [of] the motives [and purposes] of the speaker [in that situation].**

Here, each of the bracketed phrases is already implied in the others. Attempting to be precise, the writer has beclouded himself. Naturally, the speaker would be "in that situation"; naturally, a sampling of language would be "an instance" of language "in use." *Motives* may not be *purposes,* but the difference here is insignificant. Our semanticist's next sentence deserves some kind of immortality. He means "Muddy language makes trouble":

> **Unfortunately, the type of case that causes trouble in practice is that in which the kind of use made of language is not transparently clear . . . .**

Clearly, transparency is hard. Writing is hard. It requires constant attention to meanings, and constant pruning. It requires a diction a cut above the commonplace, a cut above the inaccuracies and circumlocutions of speech, yet within easy reach. Clarity is the first aim; economy, the second; grace, the third; dignity, the fourth. Our writing should be a little strange, a little out of the ordinary, a little beautiful, with words and phrases not met every day but seeming as right and natural as grass. A good diction takes care and cultivation.

It can be overcultivated. It may seem to call attention to itself rather than to its subject. Suddenly we are aware of the writer at work, and a little too pleased with himself, reaching for the elegant cliché and the showy phrase, as if he were watching his gestures in a mirror. In the following passage, I have italicized elements inoffensive, or even effective, in themselves, but horribly mannered when they get together. Some are redundant; some are trite. Everything is somehow too cozy and grandiose.

> ***There's** little excitement **ashore** when merchant ships from **far-away***

India, Nationalist China, or Egypt *knife through* the *gentle swells* of Virginia's Hampton Roads. This *unconcern* may simply reflect the *nonchalance* of people who live by *one of the world's great seaports.* Or perhaps *it's just* that *folk* who *dwell* in the *home towns* of atomic submarines and Mercury astronauts are not likely to be impressed by a visiting freighter, *from however distant a realm.*

Exercises

1. Browse your dictionary and find three families of words, like *ramp-rampage-rampant* (see p. 80). Give the root idea of each family, and a short definition of each word, using the root idea.

2. Look up in your dictionary six of the Latin and Greek constituents listed below. Illustrate each with two or three English derivatives closely translated, as in these two examples: *con-* *("with")*—*convince* (conquer with), *conclude* (shut with), *concur* (run with); *gyn-* or *gyno-* *("woman")* —*gynephobia* (fear of women), *gynecocracy* (government by women), *gynecology* (female physiology).

> LATIN: *a-* (*ab-*), *ad-*, *ante-*, *bene-*, *bi-*, *circum-*, *con-*, *contra-*, *di-* (*dis*), *e-* (*ex-*), *in-* (*two meanings*), *inter-*, *intra-*, *mal-*, *multi-*, *ob-*, *per-*, *post-*, *pre-*, *pro-*, *retro-*, *semi-*, *sub-* (*sur-*), *super-*, *trans-*, *ultra-*.

> GREEK: *a-* (*an-*), *-agogue*, *allo-*, *anthropo-*, *anti-*, *apo-*, *arch-*, *auto-*, *batho-*, *bio-*, *cata-*, *cephalo-*, *chron-*, *-cracy*, *demo-*, *dia-*, *dyna-*, *dys-*, *ecto-*, *epi-*, *eu-*, *-gen*, *geo-*, *-gon*, *-gony*, *graph-*, *gyn-*, *hemi-*, *hepta-*, *hetero-*, *hexa-*, *homo-*, *hydr-*, *hyper-*, *hypo-*, *log-*, *mega-*, *-meter*, *micro-*, *mono-*, *morph-*, *-nomy*, *-nym*, *-pathy*, *penta-*, *-phagy*, *phil-*, *-phobe* (*ia*), *-phone*, *poly-*, *pseudo-*, *psyche-*, *-scope*, *soph-*, *stero-*, *sym-* (*syn-*), *tele-*, *tetra-*, *theo-*, *thermo-*, *tri-*, *zoo-*.

3. Make three series of words running from particular to general, as in *ripe peach, peach, fruit, dessert, food, nourishment.*

4. Make three series of words running from low connotations to high (see pp. 80–81, 87–88), drawing a line (when possible) where the Anglo-Saxon gives way to French or Latin. Start with *swine* and *stuck-up* (meaning "conceited"). The abstract ideas will work best, and Roget's *Thesaurus* can be most helpful.

5. Write three sentences in which you use a concrete object to represent an entire abstract class, each sentence paired with its abstracted translation:

> A *good steak* might have saved John Keats.
> A *proper protein diet* might have saved John Keats.

6. Write three sentences in which you extend the metaphorical picture in common phrases such as *pin down, stick to, outline, count your chickens* ("She pinned him down methodically, each question sticking in a different place, until he couldn't wiggle out of it").

7. In your next essay, use a tactful *sweet as a nut, sharp as a tack,* and so forth, once on every page (see "Clichés," p. 157).

8. Write three pairs of sentences with a simile in the first sentence and its related metaphor in the second (see pp. 84–85).

9. Write three sentences in which you revive a dead metaphor.

10. Write three sentences in which you couple a Latin adjective and an Anglo-Saxon noun, as in the phrase *inconsequential snip.*

11. Write a TERRIBLE ESSAY. Have some fun with this perennial favorite, in which you reinforce your sense for clear, figurative, and meaningful words by writing the muddiest and wordiest essay you can invent, gloriously working out all your bad habits. Pick some trivial subject, like dripping faucets, and then write, in good essay form but with terribly abstract and jargonish language, *A Report of a Study of the Person Sociology and Night Loss Cost Economics of the Faucets Which Drip in the Second Floor North Corner Woman Dormitory Lavatory,* or some similarly inflated piece of nonsense. Here are the rules:

(a) Put EVERYTHING in the passive voice.
(b) Modify nouns *only* with nouns, preferably in strings of two or three, never with adjectives: *governmental spending* becomes *government cost spending;* an *excellent idea* becomes *the excellence of conception of program.*
(c) Use only big abstract nouns—as many -*tion*'s as possible.
(d) Use no participles: not *dripping faucets* but *faucets which drip;* and use as many *which*'s as possible.
(e) Use as many words as possible to say the least.
(f) Work in as many trite and wordy expressions as possible: *needless to say, all things being equal, due to the fact that, in terms of, as far as that is concerned.*
(g) Sprinkle heavily with -*wise*-type and *type*-type expressions, and say *hopefully* every three or four sentences.
(h) Compile and use a basic terrible vocabulary: *situation, aspect, function, factor, phase, utilize, the use of,* and so on. The class may well cooperate in this.

One class has had great success with a three-paragraph terrible essay, incorporating each terrible error only once, and then all rewriting the winning worst essay into the best prose possible.

9
The Research Paper

Now to consolidate and advance. Instead of a thousand words, you will write three thousand. Instead of a self-propelled debate, you will write a scholarly argument. You will also learn to use the library, and to take notes and give footnotes. You will learn the manners of scholarship. You will learn to acknowledge your predecessors as you distinguish yourself, to make not only a bibliography, but a contribution.

The research paper is very likely not what you think it is. *Re-search* is searching again. You are looking, usually, where others have looked before; but you hope to see something they have not. Research is not combining a paragraph from the *Encyclopaedia Britannica* and a paragraph from *The Book of Knowledge* with a slick pinch from *Life*. That's robbery. Nor is it research if you carefully change each phrase and acknowledge the source. That's drudgery, a kind of scavenging, what you have done in school as a "report"—sanctioned plagiarism to teach something about ants or Ankara, a tedious compiling of what is already known. That such material is new to you is not the issue: it is already in the public stock.

Choosing Your Subject

Find a thesis.

What, then, can you do, with things so well stocked? You move from facts to ideas. Here the range is infinite. Every old idea needs new assertion. Every new assertion needs judgment. Here you are in the area of values, where everyone is in favor of virtue but in doubt about what is virtuous. Your research problem is to make a judgment of right or wrong on some controversial issue.

I have put it bluntly to save you from drowning in slips of paper.

Remember that an opinion is not a private fancy; it is an opinion *about* what the right is, what the truth is, what the facts mean. It is a judgment of what *is*—out there somewhere, not merely in somebody's head. An opinion, when careful and informed, is as close as you will get to truth: a statement of what the truth of the matter seems to be. Your opinion may be just as accurate as anybody's, and the major task of the research paper is to sift opinions.

Your sifter, as always, is your thesis, right there at the funnel's neck in your beginning paragraph. Your thesis, as always, is your essay in miniature. Make your thesis first, *before you begin researching.* Call it a hypothesis (a "subthesis"), if that will make you comfortable. It does seem unscientific. But it is nearer the scientific method than it looks. The scientist, too, plays his hunches. James Watt saw the steam condenser in the lid of his aunt's teakettle; Donald Glaser saw the tracks of atomic particles in the bubbles of his beer. As with scientific experiment and the simple essay, if the hypothesis proves wrong, the testing will have furnished means to make it more nearly right. With the research paper, if you do not have a thesis to lead you through the twists and turns of print, you will never come out the other end. Unless you have a working hypothesis to keep your purpose alive as you collect, you may collect forever, forever hoping for a purpose. If you have a thesis, you will learn—and then overcome—the temptations of collecting only the supporting evidence and ignoring the obverse facts and whispers of conscience. If further facts and good arguments persuade you to the other side, so much the better. You will be the stronger for it.

Persuade your reader you are right.

You do not aim to compile mere facts. You do not aim to summarize everything ever said on the subject. You aim to persuade your reader that the thesis you believe in is right. You persuade him by: (1) letting him see that you have been thoroughly around the subject and that you know what is known of it and thought of it, (2) showing him where the wrongs are wrong, and (3) citing the rights as right. *Your* opinion, *your* thesis, is what you are showing; all your quotations from all the authorities in the world are subservient to *your* demonstration. You are the reigning authority. You have, for the moment, the longest perspective and the last word. So pick a thesis, and move into the library.

Using the Library

Start with encyclopedias.

Find the *Encyclopaedia Britannica,* and you are well on your way. The *Britannica* will survey your subject (for latest news, see latest editions, and the annual supplementary "year books"). Each article will refer you, at the end, to several authorities. If someone's initials appear at the end, look them up in the contributors' list (at the front of each volume), or in the index (the last volume of the set). The author is an authority himself; you should mention him in your paper. Furthermore, the contributors' list will name several works, which will swell your bibliography and aid your research. The index will also refer you to data scattered through all the volumes. Under "Medicine," for instance, it directs you to such topics as "Academies," "Hypnotism," "Licensing," "Mythology," and so on. Since the *Britannica* now revises progressively, subject by subject, note the date on the copyright page to see how much you may need to bring your subject up to date. The *Encyclopedia Americana* and *Collier's Encyclopedia,* though less celebrated, will here and there challenge *Britannica's* reign. Others will help:

The American Yearbook
Catholic Encyclopedia
Columbia Encyclopedia
Dictionary of American Biography [abbreviated *DAB* in footnotes]
Dictionary of American History
Dictionary of Music and Musicians
Dictionary of National Biography [British—abbreviated *DNB* in footnotes]
Dictionary of Philosophy and Psychology
Encyclopedia of Religion and Ethics
Encyclopedia of the Social Sciences
Encyclopedia of World Art
Encyclopedia of World History
Harper's Encyclopedia of Art
Jewish Encyclopedia
McGraw-Hill Encyclopedia of Science and Technology
Who's Who [British]
Who's Who in America

The World Almanac and Book of Facts, a paperbacked mine of news and statistics (issued yearly since 1868), can provide a factual nugget for almost any subject. The *Interpreter's Dictionary of the Bible* is another gold mine.

Next find the card catalog.

Its 3 × 5 cards list all the library's holdings—books, magazines, newspapers, atlases—and alphabetize (1) authors, (2) publications, and (3) general subjects, from *A* to *Z*. You will find *John Adams* and *The Anatomy of Melancholy* and *Atomic Energy*, in that order, in the *A* drawers. The next page illustrates the three kinds of cards (filed alphabetically) on which the card catalog will list the same book—by author, by subject, and by title.

You will notice that the bottom of the card shows the Library of Congress's cataloging number (Q175.W6517) and the number from the older, but still widely used, Dewey Decimal System (501). Your library will use one or the other, to make its own "call number," typed in the upper left corner of its cards—the number you will put on your slip when you sign out the book.

Learn the catalog's inner arrangements.

Since some alphabetical entries run on, drawer after drawer —*New York City, New York Times, New York State*, for instance— knowing the arrangements *within* these entries will help you find your book.

1. Not only men, but organizations and institutions, can be "authors" if they publish books or magazines, as do the following:

Parke, Davis & Company, Detroit
The University of Michigan
U.S. Department of State

2. Initial *A, An, The,* and their foreign equivalents (*Ein, El, Der, Une,* and so forth) are ignored in alphabetizing a title: *A Long Day in a Short Life* is alphabetized under *L*. But French surnames are treated as if they were one word: *De la Mare* as if *Delamare, La Rochefoucauld* as if *Larochefoucauld*.

3. Cards are usually alphabetized *word by word: Stock Market* comes before *Stockard* and *Stockbroker*. "Short before long" is another way of putting it, meaning that *Stock* and all its combinations with separate words precede the longer words beginning with *Stock-*. Hy-

Author Card:
The "Main Entry"

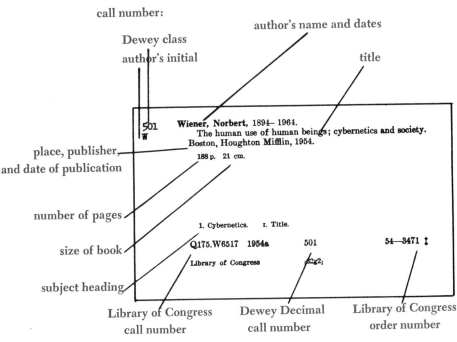

call number:
Dewey class
author's initial

author's name and dates

title

501
W

Wiener, Norbert, 1894– 1964.
The human use of human beings; cybernetics and society.
Boston, Houghton Mifflin, 1954.
188 p. 21 cm.

place, publisher,
and date of publication

number of pages

size of book

subject heading

1. Cybernetics.   I. Title.

Q175.W6517 1954a   501   54—3471

Library of Congress   [62g2]

Library of Congress
call number

Dewey Decimal
call number

Library of Congress
order number

Subject Card

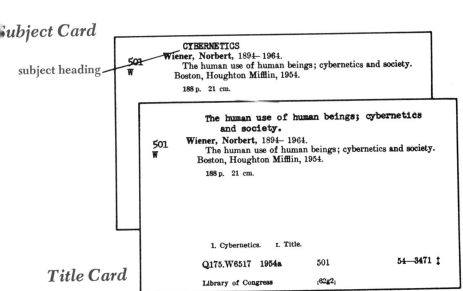

subject heading

CYBERNETICS
Wiener, Norbert, 1894– 1964.
The human use of human beings; cybernetics and society.
Boston, Houghton Mifflin, 1954.
188 p. 21 cm.

501
W

The human use of human beings; cybernetics
and society.
Wiener, Norbert, 1894– 1964.
The human use of human beings; cybernetics and society.
Boston, Houghton Mifflin, 1954.
188 p. 21 cm.

501
W

1. Cybernetics.   I. Title.

Q175.W6517 1954a   501   54—3471

Library of Congress   [62g2]

Title Card

phenated compounds are treated as two words. The sequence would run thus:

Stock
Stock-Exchange Rulings
Stock Market
Stockard

4. Cards on one subject are arranged alphabetically by author. Under *Anatomy*, for instance, you will run from *Abernathy, John* to *Yutzy, Simon Menno*, and then suddenly run into a title—*An Anatomy of Conformity*—which happens to be the next large alphabetical item after the subject *Anatomy*.

5. Identical names are arranged in the order (a) persons, (b) titles and places, as they fall alphabetically:

Washington, Booker T.
Washington, George
Washington (State)
Washington, D.C.
Washington, University of
Washington Square [by Henry James]

Washington the state precedes the other *Washington*'s because "State" (which appears on the card only in parentheses) is not treated as part of its name.

6. Since *Mc, M'*, and *Mac* are all filed as *Mac*, go by the letter following them: *M'Coy, McDermott, Machinery, MacKenzie*.

7. Other abbreviations are also filed as if spelled out: *Dr. Zhivago* would be filed as if beginning with *Doctor; St.* as if *Saint; Mrs. Miniver* as if *Mistress*—except that many libraries now alphabetize *Mr.* and *Mrs.* as spelled.

8. Saints, popes, kings, and people are filed, in that order, by name and not by appellation (do not look under *Saint* for Saint Paul, nor under *King* for King Henry VIII):

Paul, Saint
Paul VI, Pope
Paul I, Emperor of Russia
Paul, Jean

9. An author's books are filed first by collected works, then by individual titles. Different editions of the same title follow chronologically. Books *about* an author follow the books *by* him.

That is the system. Now you can thumb through the cards filed under your subject—"Cancer," or "Television," or "Hawthorne"—to see what books your library has on it, and you can look up any authorities your encyclopedia has mentioned. Two or three of the most recent books will probably give you all you want, because each of these will refer you, by footnote and bibliography, to important previous works.

Check the indexes.

The card catalog will give you the books on your subject. The indexes will give you the magazine articles. Begin with the *Readers' Guide to Periodical Literature*—an index of articles (and portraits and poems) in more than one hundred magazines. Again, take the most recent issue, look up your subject, and make yourself a bibliographical card for each title—spelling out the abbreviations of titles and dates according to the key just inside the cover. If you don't spell them out fully, your cards may be mysteries to you when you sit down to write. You can drop back a few issues and years to collect more articles; and if your subject belongs to the recent past (after 1907), you can drop back to the right year and track your subject forward.

You can do the same with *The New York Times Index*, beginning with 1913. It will probably lead you to news that appeared in any paper. The *Social Sciences and Humanities Index* does for the scholarly journals what the *Readers' Guide* does for the popular ones. Add to these the *Book Review Digest* and the *Biography Index* (which nicely collects scattered references), and you will probably need no more. But here are some others:

Annual Magazine Subject-Index [particularly for history]
Art Index
Dramatic Index
Education Index
Engineering Index
Essay and General Literature Index [very useful for locating particular subjects within collections of essays]
Index Medicus
International Catalogue of Scientific Literature
Music Index
Psychological Index
Public Affairs Information Service [valuable for "current events" beginning with October 15, 1914]
Technical Book Review Index

If you need more, consult Constance M. Winchell's *Guide to Reference Books.*

Making Your Cards

Make your bibliography as you go.

Even before you start toward the library, get some 3 × 5 cards for your bibliography. Plan on some ten or fifteen sources for your three thousand words of text. As you pick up an author or two, and some titles, start a bibliographical card for each: *one card for each title.* Leave space to the left to put in the call number later, and space at the top for a label of your own, if needed. Put the author (last name first) on one line, and the title of his work on the next, leaving space to fill in the details of publication when you get to the work itself— for books, place of publication, publisher, and date; for magazine articles, volume number, date, and pages. Italicize (that is, underscore) titles of books and magazines; put titles of articles *within* books and magazines in quotation marks. The card catalog will supply the call numbers, and much of the other publishing data you need; but check and complete all your publishing data when you finally get the book or magazine in your hands, putting a light √ in pencil to assure yourself that your card is authoritative, safe to check your finished paper against. Get the author's name as he signed it, adding details in brackets, if helpful: Smith, D[elmar] P[rince]. Get all the information, to save repeated trips to the library. The completed cards and bibliography with our sample paper (pp.114, 116, 127–128) will show you what you need.

Take few notes.

Some people abhor putting notes on bibliographical cards. But the economy is well worth the slight clutter. Limiting yourself to what you can put on the front and back of one bibliographical card will restrain your notes to the sharp and manageable. You can always add another note card, or a 3 × 5 slip of paper, if you must. If you find one source offering a number of irresistible quotations, put each one separately on a 3 × 5 slip (with author's name on each), so you can rearrange them later for writing.

However you do it, keep your notes brief. Read quickly, with an eye for the general idea and the telling point. Holding a clear thesis in mind will guide and limit your note taking. Some of your sources will need no more than the briefest summary: "Violently opposed, recommends complete abolition." This violent and undistinguished author will appear in your paper only among several others in a single footnote to one of your sentences: "Opposition, of course, has been long and emphatic.²"

Suppose you are writing a paper to show (as the student author of our sample paper actually did) that Hawthorne's *The Scarlet Letter* is historically inaccurate. You find an article (Baughman's—see the first card and first footnote, below, pp. 114–115) that asserts Hawthorne's historicity. Here is a perfect piece of opposition, a *con*, to set your thesis against. But don't copy down too much. Summarize the author's points briefly in your own words, and copy down directly, within distinct quotation marks, only the most quotable phrases: "was on sure historical grounds at all times." Add the page number in parentheses. Then verify your copying against the text, word for word, comma for comma, and give it a penciled check when you know it is accurate.

Take care with page numbers. When your passage runs from one page to the next—from 29 over onto 30, for instance—put "(29–30)" after it, but also mark the exact point where the page changed. You might want to use only part of the passage and then be uncertain as to which of the two pages contained it. An inverted L-bracket and the number "30" after the last word of page 29, will do nicely: see the bottom card on page 116. Do the same even when the page changes in mid-word with a hyphen: "having con- $\lceil$²⁶ vinced no one."

In a research paper on a piece of literature, like our Hawthorne paper, you would also make a bibliographical card for the edition you are using, and would probably need a number of note slips for summaries and quotations from the work itself—one slip for each item, for convenience in sorting. Here again, check for accuracy of quotation and page number, probably identified in the lower right corner as "Hawthorne 213," or "SL 213," for page 213 in *The Scarlet Letter*. Our sample bibliographical card (p. 116) does not need a call number because *The Portable Hawthorne* was the student's textbook.

The First Draft

Plot your course.

Formal outlines, especially those made too early in the game, can take more time than they are worth, but a long paper with notes demands some planning. First, draft a beginning paragraph, incorporating your thesis. Then read through your notes, arranging them roughly in the order you think you will use them, getting the opposition off the street first. If your thesis is strongly argumentative, you can sort into three piles: *pro's*, *con's*, and *in-between's* (often simple facts). Now, by way of outline, you can simply make three or four general headings on a sheet of paper, with ample space between, in which you can jot down your sources in the order, *pro* and *con*, that is best for your argument. Our Hawthorne paper would block out something like this:

I. Hawthorne's historical claims

PRO	CON
	Custom House
	Text
	Early refs to scarlet A

II. The critics

	Baughman
But—Green	
Trollope	
	H's own belief
But—Schwartz	
Waggoner	
Kaul	

III. Actual historical content

	H's "religion and law"
	Page Smith—confession

IV. Unhistorical details

But—courts and church later
H's dating—before 1650
Hester's treatment
 (Lawrence, Nettels, Morgan, Winthrop's journal, Smith)
Dimmesdale
 (Smith)
Chillingworth

Outline more fully, if you wish.

You can easily refine this rough blocking (probably more nearly complete here than yours would actually be) into a full topic outline, one that displays your points logically, not necessarily in the actual sequence of your writing (see p. 113). The principle of outlining is to rank equivalent headings—keeping your headings all as nouns, or noun phrases, to make the ranks apparent. You simply mark heads and subheads by alternating numbers and letters as you proceed downhill, from roman numeral *I* through capital *A* to arabic *1* and lowercase *a*, until you reach, if you need them, parenthesized *(1)* and *(a)*, and even lowercase roman numerals *i, ii, iii*, as your very smallest subdivisions. You indent equal heads equally, aligning equivalents under equivalents, roman under roman, capital under capital, and so on. Every *A* should have its *B*, at least; and every *1* its *2*. If you have just a single heading, drop it, or absorb it into the larger heading above it.

Begin to write soon.

You have already begun to write, of course, in getting your thesis down on paper, and then drafting a first paragraph to hold it. Now that you have blocked out your argument, however roughly, plunge into your first draft. Your ideas will have been well warmed. Don't let them cool too long. Settle down to the keyboard and begin your second paragraph.

Put in your references as you go.

Your first draft should have all your footnotes, abbreviated, right in the text. Otherwise you will lose your place, and go mad with numbers. Put the notes at the *end* of the last pertinent sentence, with as many of your references as possible grouped in one note. Make your quotations in full, all distinctly set within quotation marks, and include the author's surname and the page number with each citation. You will change these in your final draft, of course, filling in the names or leaving them out of the note altogether if they appear in the text. But it will help you in checking against your cards to have an author's name and a page number for each citation. *Don't number your footnotes yet.* When your draft is finished, add the numbers in pencil, so you can change them; circle them in red pencil, so you can see them. As you type along, mark your notes with triple parentheses: (((. . .)))— the easiest distinction you can make. See page 118 for a sample first-draft page, with its accompanying transformation into smooth and final copy.

Your Final Draft

Reset your long quotations.

Your final draft will change in many ways, as the rewriting polishes up your phrases and turns up new and better ideas. But some changes are merely presentational. The triple parentheses of your first draft will disappear, along with the quotation marks around the *long* quotations. You will single-space and indent, *without quotation marks,* all quotations of more than fifty words, to simulate the appearance of a printed page. You will do the same with shorter quotations, if you want to give them special emphasis, and also with passages of poetry. If your quotation begins as a paragraph, indent its first line further, to reproduce the paragraphing. Again, pages 118–120 show how a first-draft quotation is transformed in the final draft. Check the rules about quotation marks on pages 28 and 74–75.

Allow space for notes at the foot of the page.

Some instructors like footnotes gathered all together in a section at the end, as they would be in a manuscript prepared for the printer (see p. 110). But most prefer them at the foot, where you can see them, as if on a printed page. From your preliminary draft, you can see about how many footnotes will fall on your page, and about how much space to allow at the bottom. Allow plenty. You will begin your notes three spaces below your text. You have been double-spacing your text; now triple-space. Do *not* type a line between text and notes: this indicates a footnote continued from the preceding page. Single-space each note, but double-space between notes. Indent as for a paragraph. To type the number, use the variable line spacer and roll down about half the height of a capital letter. After typing the number, return to your normal typing line: [16]Smith, p. 62. After the first line, notes run out to the left margin, as in paragraphs.

Footnotes carry only information not mentioned in the text. At first mention in text or note, give your author's full name, in normal order—"Ernest W. Baughman"—and use only his last name thereafter. (Your alphabetized bibliography will give last name first.) If your text names the author, the note carries only the title of his work, the publishing data, and the page number. If your text names the author and his work, the note carries only the publishing data and the page number. Once you have cited a source, you can put the page numbers of further citations directly in your text, within parentheses. Note where the periods and the quotation marks go:

> Baughman states that Hawthorne was familiar with John Winthrop's journals and other Puritan documents (p. 539).
>
> . . . what Kaul refers to as "the interpretative Puritan myth" (p. 9).

At the end of a long indented, single-spaced quotation from a work already cited, the page number in parentheses *follows* the period (see example on p. 125):

> . . . God's forgiveness as inexhaustible. (p. 63)

Make and punctuate your footnotes meticulously.
The three principle kinds of reference produce three forms of footnotes:

BOOK

[1] Malcolm Cowley, *The Portable Hawthorne* (New York: Viking Press, 1948), p. 269.

QUARTERLY MAGAZINE

[2] Ernest W. Baughman, "Public Confession and *The Scarlet Letter*," *The New England Quarterly*, 40 (1967), 548–549.

> [When giving the volume number, "40," you omit the "p." or "pp." before page numbers, which I prefer in full. If you choose to abbreviate them, do it thus: "548–49," not "548–9"; "27–29," not "27–9"; but "107–8," not "107–08." Convert all roman volume numbers into arabic: "XL" becomes "40."]

POPULAR MAGAZINE

[3] J. J. Uptight, "Swinging Puritans," *Saturday Night Journal*, Sept. 30, 1984, p. 5.

> [Ignore volume number, if any.]

As in this last example, give the full date for a popular magazine, instead of volume number and year, and *use no parentheses.* Newspaper articles follow the same pattern:

[4] "The Trouble with Puritans" (editorial), *New York Times*, April 10, 1984, Sec. 4, p. 8.

> [Notice the comma here: omitted after "Puritans" and inserted after the parenthesis. Do the same with any parenthetical explanation of a title. With this newspaper, you need to give the section number because each section begins numbering anew.]

Here are some further complications:

[5] Abraham B. Caldwell, "The Case for a Puritan Revival," *American Questioner*, June 20, 1971, p. 37, quoted in Albert N. Mendenhall, *The Time Is Now* (Princeton: Little House, 1969), p. 308.

> [You have found the quotation in Mendenhall's book.]

[6] D. C. Hill, "Who Is Communicating What?" in *Essays for Study*, ed. James L. McDonald and Leonard P. Doan (New York: Appleton Hall, 1973), p. 214; reprinted from *Era*, 12 (1972).

> [McDonald and Doan have edited the collection, or case-book. A title ending in a question mark should not take a comma.]

[7] David R. Small, "The Telephone and Urbanization," in *Annals of American Communication*, ed. Walter Beinholt (Boston: Large, Green and Co., 1969), III, 401.

> [The *Annals of American Communication* is a series of bound books, not a magazine: the volume number is in roman numerals, and it *follows* the parenthesis. Had this been a magazine, the entry would have omitted the "in," the editor, and the place of publication, and would have read ". . . *Annals of American Communication*, 3 (1969), 401."]

[8] Arnold Peters, "Medicine," *Encyc. Brit.*, 11th ed.

> [Abbreviate familiar titles, so long as they remain clear. You need neither volume nor page numbers in alphabetized encyclopedias; and only the number (*or* the year of publication) of the edition you are citing, without parentheses. Here the article was initialed "A. P.," and you have looked up the author's name in the contributors' list.]

[9] "Prunes," *Encyc. Brit.*, 11th ed.

> [Here the article was not initialed.]

[10] George L. Gillies, "Robert Herrick's 'Corinna,'" *Speculation*, 2 (1881), 490.

> [This shows where to put the comma when the title of a magazine article ends in a quotation, and you have to use both single and double quotation marks. Gillies's original title would have looked like this: Robert Herrick's "Corinna."]

[11] *Romeo and Juliet* II.iii.94, in *An Essential Shakespeare*, ed. Russell Fraser (New York: Prentice-Hall, 1972).

[Note the absence of the comma after the play's title, and the periods and close spacing between Act.scene.line. Subsequent references would go directly in your text within parentheses: "(IV.iii.11–12)." Or, if you are quoting several of Shakespeare's plays: "(*Romeo* IV.iii.11–12)." See further instructions below.]

¹² P[aul] F[riedrich] Schwartz, *A Quartet of Thoughts* (New York: Appleton Hall, 1943), p. 7.

¹³ [Lewes, George H.], "Percy Bysshe Shelley," *Westminster Review*, 35 (April 1841), 303–344.

[These two footnotes show how to use brackets to add details not actually appearing in the published work. Of course, famous initials are kept as initials, as with T. S. Eliot, H. G. Wells, or D. H. Lawrence.]

¹⁴ "The Reading Problem," mimeographed pamphlet, Concerned Parents Committee, Center City, Arkansas, Dec. 25, 1973, p. 8.

¹⁵ U. S. Congress, House Committee on Health, Education, and Welfare, *Racial Integration*, 101st Cong., 2nd sess., 1969, H. Rep. 391 to accompany H. R. 6128.

[These represent the infinite variety of pamphlets, and other oddities, that may contain just the information you want. These you must play by instinct, including all the details that would help someone else hunt them down, as briefly as possible.]

These examples, together with the footnotes in our sample research paper, should cover most footnoting problems, or suggest how you can meet them.

Abbreviate your references after the first full citation.

Two old favorite abbreviations are now mercifully out of style. Do NOT USE:

ibid.—*ibidem* ("in the same place"), meaning the title cited in the note directly before. Instead, USE THE AUTHOR'S LAST NAME, AND GIVE THE PAGE.

op. cit.—*opere citato* ("in the work cited"), meaning a title referred to again after other notes have intervened. Again, USE THE AUTHOR'S LAST NAME INSTEAD, AND GIVE THE PAGE: "Smith, p. 62." If you have two Smiths, simply include their initials. If Smith has two articles or books on the Puritans, devise two convenient short titles for subsequent references:

[2] Smith, *City*, p. 62.
[3] Smith, "Puritan Souls," p. 301.

Four are still used and especially useful (do *not* italicize them):

cf.—*confer* ("compare"); do not use for "see."

et al.—*et alii* ("and others"); does not mean "and all"; use after the first author in multiple authorships: "Ronald Elkins, et al."

loc. cit.—*loco citato* ("in the place cited"); use without page number, when you cite a page previously noted. Best in parentheses *in the text*. See page 115, toward the bottom.

passim—(not an abbreviation, but a Latin word meaning "throughout the work; here and there"); use when a writer makes the same point in many places within a single work; use also for statistics you have compiled from observations and tables scattered throughout his work.

Other useful abbreviations for footnotes are:

c. or ca.	*circa,* "about" (c. 1709)
ch., chs.	chapter, chapters
ed.	edited by, edition, editor
f., ff.	and the following page, pages
l., ll.	line, lines
MS., MSS.	manuscript, manuscripts
n.d.	no date given
n.p.	no place of publication given
p., pp.	page, pages
rev.	revised
tr., trans.	translated by
vol., vols.	volume, volumes

A footnote using some of these might go like this (you have already fully cited Weiss and Dillon):

[16] See Donald Allenberg, et al., *Population in Early New England* (Boston: Large, Green and Co., 1974), pp. 308 ff.; cf. Weiss, p. 60. Dillon, passim, takes a position even more conservative than Weiss's. See also A. H. Hawkins, ed., *Statistical Surveys* (Chicago: Nonesuch Press, 1960; rev. 1973), pp. 71–83 and ch. 10. Records sufficient for broad comparisons begin only ca. 1850.

Abbreviate books of the Bible, even the first time.

The Bible and its books, though capitalized as ordinary titles, are never italicized. Biblical references go directly into your text, within parentheses—no footnote, no commas, *lowercase* roman numerals for chapter, arabic for verse: "Mark xvi.6"; "Jer. vi.24"; "II Sam. xviii.33." No comma—only a space—separates name from numbers; periods separate the numbers, *with no spacing.* The dictionary gives the accepted abbreviations: Gen., Exod., Lev., Deut. Make biblical references like this:

> **There is still nothing new under the sun (Eccl. i.9); man still does not live by bread alone (Matt. iv.4).**
>
> **As Ecclesiastes tells us, "there is no new thing under the sun" (i.9).**

Abbreviate plays and long poems after the first time.

Handle plays and long poems like biblical citations, after an initial footnote that identifies the edition (see pp. 106–107). Italicize the title: "*Merch.* II iv.72–75" (this is *The Merchant of Venice*, Act II, Scene iv, lines 72–75); "*Caesar* V.iii.6," "*Ham.* I.i.23," "*Iliad* IX.93," "*P.L.* IV.918" (*Paradise Lost*, Book IV, line 918). Use the numbers alone if you have already mentioned the title, or have clearly implied it, as in repeated quotations from the same work.

Match your bibliography to your footnotes.

When your paper is finally typed, arrange the cards of the works cited in your footnotes in alphabetical order (by authors' last names or, with anonymous works, by first words of titles—ignoring initial *The, A,* or *An*). You will not have used all your notes, nor all the articles you have carded. In typing your bibliography, pass over them in decent silence. *Include no work not specifically cited.* Your bibliographical entries will be just like your footnotes except that: (1) you will put the author's last name first; (2) you will give the total span of pages for magazine articles—none at all for books; (3) you will reverse indentation so that the author's name will stand out; (4) you will punctuate differently—putting one period after the alphabetized name or title, and another (no parentheses) after a book's place and date of publication; and (5) you will double-space, triple-spacing between entries. Your single-spacing of footnotes has been the typewriter's approximation of passages set in small print. If you had been actually writing for print, you would have double-spaced everything and would not have put your footnotes at the bottoms of pages: you would have collected them serially at the end of the paper in a section headed "Footnotes," so that the printer could conveniently set the notes in smaller type all at the same time. In many publications you would not have a bibliography; in many others, you would. Your research paper usually requires one, like that with our sample paper (pp. 127–128). Here are some special cases:

Hill, D. C. "Who Is Communicating What?" in *Essays for Study,* ed. James L. McDonald and Leonard P. Doan. New York: Appleton Hall, 1973. Pp. 211–219. Reprinted from *Era,* 12 (1972), 9–18.
> [Notice the capitalized "Pp. 211–219." Since this article is in a book, the publishing data have required a period after "1973."]

Jones, Bingham. *The Kinescopic Arts and Sciences.* Princeton: Little House, 1970.

————. "Television and Vision: The Case for Governmental Control," *Independent Review,* 7 (1969), 18–31.
> [When listing other works by the same author, use a solid line (your underscorer) and a period.]

Small, David R. "The Telephone and Urbanization," in *Annals of American Communication,* ed. Walter Beinholt. Boston: Large, Green and Co., 1969. III, 398–407.

"The Trouble with Puritans." Anon. editorial, *New York Times,* April 10, 1968, Sec. 4, p. 8.

I have based these instructions on *The MLA Style Sheet* (compiled by the Modern Language Association of America) and Kate L. Turabian, *A Manual for Writers of Term Papers, Theses, and Dissertations,* following the customs for work in literature and the humanities. The sciences use slightly different conventions. Bingham Jones's article would look like this in a botanical bibliography (no italics, no quotation marks, no parentheses):

Television and Vision: The Case for Governmental Control. Independent Review.8:8–31.

For some advanced courses, you may also want to consult:

McCrum, Blanche, and Helen Jones. *Bibliographical Procedures & Style: A Manual for Bibliographers in the Library of Congress.* Washington, D.C.: Superintendent of Documents, 1954.

Publication Manual of the American Psychological Association. Washington, D.C.,'1957.

Style Manual. U.S. Government Printing Office. Rev. ed. Washington, D.C., 1959.

Style Manual for Biological Journals. Washington, D.C., 1960.

Wood, George McLane. *Suggestions to Authors . . . , United States Geological Survey.* 4th ed. rev. by Bernard H. Lane. Washington, D.C., 1935.

Follow the conventional format.

Since the full-dress research paper usually has four parts, here is a checklist for your convenience:

I. Title Page (not numbered) *

    A. In the upper half, centered on the page, type your title in capitals, and beneath it, your name.

    B. In the lower third, designate on separate lines, also centered, the course and section, your instructor's name, and the date.

II. Outline (page not numbered unless it runs to more than one; if so, use lowercase roman numerals: i, ii, iii, iv)

    A. Head the page with your title.

    B. State your thesis in a sentence.

    C. Present your outline—topic or sentence as your instructor specifies. (Remember that the headings of a sentence outline— like your thesis, which is always a complete sentence—end in a period, but those of a topic outline do not.) It will serve as your paper's table of contents.

III. Text with Footnotes (pages numbered in arabic numerals from first to last)

    A. After heading the first page with your title, type your text double-spaced –except for long quotations, which you indent and single-space, without quotation marks, to simulate smaller print.

    B. Type your footnotes at the bottom of your text pages, each single-spaced, but with a space between notes, and in proper form (see pp. 105–109). Or your instructor may ask you to group all your footnotes together following the text, beginning on a new page headed "Footnotes," and continuing the page numbering of the text.

---

* Some instructors do not require a separate title page. Our sample research paper (p. 113) will show you how to set up your first page to combine the title and the outline. Either way, the page is not numbered unless the outline runs to more than one page (see "Outline" section of this checklist).

IV. Bibliography (pages numbered in continuation of text paging)
   A. Head the first page "Bibliography" or "Works Cited."
   B. Arrange the works in one of two ways: (1) alphabetized, by author's last name (Eliot, T. S.), and by title when the author is unknown ("Medicine," *Encyclopaedia Britannica*); or (2) grouped by kind of source, the entries within each group arranged alphabetically: "Primary Sources" (works of literature, historical documents, letters, and the like) and "Secondary Sources" (works *about* your subject)—and you may further divide these groups, if your bibliography is long enough to justify it, into "Books" and "Articles."

Sample Paper

Here is a sample, a complete research paper (an exceptionally good one, from one of my classes), to show what the final product can look like. This paper started from our reading and discussing Nathaniel Hawthorne's novel *The Scarlet Letter*. As you can see, the student author, a history major, brought her personal interests nicely to bear on a literary subject. You can follow this sample paper throughout for customs of typing and spacing. To convey an idea of the whole process, the backs of the first three pages show bibliographical cards with notes corresponding to the first four footnotes, and a page of the first draft, which matches the text it faces at the line (mid-page) beginning "about the difficulty of writing . . . ."

Marilyn Ferris
English 269
Mr. Baker
April 16, 1973

HAWTHORNE'S PURITANS

Thesis: Despite its moral power and claims to authenticity,

The Scarlet Letter is historically untrue.

  I.   Hawthorne's claims of historical accuracy
       A.   The "Custom House" introduction
       B.   Phrases in the text implying historical accuracy
       C.   Hawthorne's prior references to a scarlet "A"
            1.   "Endicott and the Red Cross"
            2.   Entry in notebook

 II.   The critical estimate
       A.   Baughman's assertion "sure of historical grounds"
       B.   Green's attack
       C.   Trollope's view as "romance"
       D.   Hawthorne's own belief
            1.   Entry in notebook: "old colony law"
            2.   Schwartz's evidence
            3.   Waggoner's analysis
            4.   Kaul's comment on archaism
       E.   Hawthorne's "Puritan myth"

III.   Hawthorne's actual use of history
       A.   Union of religion and law
       B.   The Puritan's idea of community
       C.   Isolation by sin
       D.   Reunion by confession and repentence

 IV.   Hawthorne's unique characters
       A.   Hester
            1.   Hester's alienation
                 a.   Resistance to community
                 b.   Impenitence
            2.   Hester's independent solution
       B.   Dimmesdale
       C.   Chillingworth

  V.   Hawthorne's projecting unique cases from general Puritan
       practices, and making them universal

front

F   Baughman, Ernest W.
1   "Public Confession and _The Scarlet Letter_,"
N4   _New England Quarterly_, 40 (1967),
       532-550. ✓

Public confession, an English custom—required by
church and state in Mass. Bay Colony from
its founding on, in Plymouth from 1624, in Va.
at least 30 years before _SL_ takes place. (533)

H. familiar with John Winthrop's _Journals_,

---

back

1630-1650. W. records 16 pub. confessions, 4
  for adultery. (539)

Hester not reunited w. community because she refuses
to repent and name her partner. (544)

Hawthorne "was on sure historical grounds at all
times." (548) He uses custom of confession of sins
that isolate "from the fellowship of the church."
(544) Characterization consistent w. Puritan thought
"though, until the end, much of their conduct
is at odds w. the tradition." (549)

---

single entry

813   Levin, David
S 816   "Nathaniel Hawthorne, _The Scarlet Letter_,"
         in _The American Novel from James
         Fenimore Cooper to Wm Faulkner_, ed.
         Wallace Stegner (New York: Basic
         Books, 1965), pp. 13-24. ✓

"... he studied Puritan history w. a persistence
that some scholars (along with H. himself)
have considered obsessive." (13)

HAWTHORNE'S PURITANS

In _The Scarlet Letter_, Hawthorne presents the system of
ethics, law, and punishment in a Puritan New England town. He
introduces his story of adultery and expiation with an elaborate
account of finding a faded red-cloth "A" twisted around a roll of
papers, among other documents in the Salem Custom House, which he
intends to give to the Essex Historical Society. The roll of
papers contains, in "Surveyor Pue's" handwriting, the story of
Hester Prynne. In the narrative itself, Hawthorne makes numerous
other assertions of historical fact. But all of this is fiction.
Actually, _The Scarlet Letter_, though generally acknowledged as a
great moral novel, is historically untrue.

Ernest W. Baughman, however, claims that Hawthorne "was on
sure historical grounds at all times," because he employs the
Puritan idea that public confession reunites the sinner with the
community.[1] Baughman concedes that "until the end, much of [the]
conduct is at odds with the tradition," but he insists that the
essential characterization and the underlying idea are historically faithful (loc. cit.). Baughman states that Hawthorne was
familiar with John Winthrop's journals and other Puritan documents (p. 539). According to David Levin, Hawthorne "studied

[1]"Public Confession and _The Scarlet Letter_," _New England
Quarterly_, 40 (1967), 548-549.

Cowley, Malcolm
   The *Portable Hawthorne*, ed., with Introduction
   and Notes, by Malcolm Cowley (New York:
   Viking Press, 1948). ✓

Character wearing "the letter A on the breast of
her gown" appears in 1 sentence, "Endicott
and the Red Cross." pub. 1837 – first hint
of *SL* . (269)
Seven yrs. later, in one of H.'s note books is

front

" plot of a new story he planned to write:
   'The life of a woman who, by the old colony
   law, was condemned always to wear the
   letter A, sewed on her garment, in token
   of her having committed adultery.' " (269)

back

820.6   Green, Martin
E58r   "The Hawthorne Myth: A Protest," *Essays and*
      Studies by Members of the English Association,
      16 (1963), 16-36. ✓

"T.S. Eliot has said that H.'s is a true criticism of
the Puritan morality, true because it has the
fidelity of the artist & not a mere conviction of the
man, but there is very little that is Puritan in *The SL*.
The thoughts and emotions expressed all belong to [30] the
nineteenth century" (29-30) Claims "to be historical
are so insistent and so unacceptable..." (29)

all on one side

Puritan history with a persistence that some scholars (along with Hawthorne himself) have considered obsessive."[2]

But the evidence undermines Hawthorne's claims of factuality. First, a character wearing a "letter A on [her] breast" appears briefly in an early Hawthorne story ("Endicott and the Red Cross," 1837); then seven years later and six years before he started The Scarlet Letter, Hawthorne records in his notebook plans to write: "The life of a woman, who, by the old colony law, was condemned always to wear the letter A, sewed on her garment, in token of her having committed adultery."[3] Hawthorne mentions discovering no manuscript and faded letter, and such a discovery would certainly have been exciting news, to be recorded in his notebook and in letters to his friends. He records no such discovery. Clearly, his "document," and his claims of finding it, are fictitious, if not fraudulent.

Martin Green is the severest of Hawthorne's critics. He sets aside T. S. Eliot's claim that Hawthorne's picture of Puritan morality is true "because it has the fidelity of the artist." The book's claims to historicity, says Green, are "so insistent and so unacceptable": ". . . there is very little that is Puritan in The Scarlet Letter. The thoughts and emotions all belong to

[2]"Nathaniel Hawthorne, The Scarlet Letter," in The American Novel from James Fenimore Cooper to William Faulkner, ed. Wallace Stegner (New York: Basic Books, 1965), p. 13.

[3]Malcolm Cowley, The Portable Hawthorne (New York: Viking Press, 1948), p. 269.

of writing ~~entertaining and~~ lively children's stories ~~for children~~ with

"such unmaleable material as the somber, stern, and rigid

Puritans," ((("Three Aspects of Hawthorne's Puritanism," The

New England Quarterly, 36 (1936), 202.))) ~~He also~~ noting that

Hawthorne consistently ~~looked upon~~ viewed his Puritan ancestors as

"gloomy, joyless, and rigid." (((Schwartz, loc. cit.))) Appar-

ently Hawthorne's view of the Puritans distorted his picture of the past ~~was distorted~~. As Hyatt

H. Waggoner puts it: "Despite his long absorption in Puritan

writings, it is pretty clear that Hawthorne had a typical

nineteenth-century view of his ancestors. He exaggerated their

gloominess and their intolerance and probably attributed their

persecution of sexual offenses to ideas other than those they

actually held." (((Hawthorne, A Critical Study (Cambridge: Harvard University Press,

1963), p. 14))) As A. N. Kaul says, "This archaism appears to have

been a necessary condition for the richest engagement of his

imagination, and also, paradoxically, for his deepest intuitions

of the modern spirit." ((("Introduction," Hawthorne: A Collection

of Critical Essays (Englewood Cliffs: Prentice-Hall, 1966), p. 2.)))

But we must concede that ~~Of course~~, Hawthorne ~~does~~ follows historical facts ~~history~~, at least part of

the way ~~time~~. As he states in Chapter 2, the Puritans were in fact

"a people amongst whom ~~and~~ religion and law were almost iden-

tical." Page Smith ~~in his book As a City Upon a Hill, tells~~ reports that ~~about how~~ the early Puritans were forced to confess their sins

before the entire congregation, which consisted of almost the

entire population of the town. The penitent sinner ~~who was penitent~~ was

then accepted ~~taken~~ back into the congregation, but the impenitent sinner ~~who was~~

not was excommunicated, regardless of the relative mildness of ~~how mild~~ his sin ~~was~~.

the nineteenth century."[4] Of course, Hawthorne called his book
"A Romance" on the title page. Anthony Trollope, writing in 1879,
is probably typical of Hawthorne's readers in accepting the historical pretense as a usual part of fiction: "His is a mixture
of romance and austerity, quite as far removed from the realities
of Puritanism as it is from the sentimentalism of poetry."[5]

Nevertheless, in spite of the fictional deceit of the Custom
House introduction, Hawthorne himself probably thought he was
more historically accurate than Trollope allows. His statement
in his notebook about "the old colony law" shows his belief in
its authenticity. Joseph Schwartz quotes Hawthorne's complaint
about the difficulty of writing lively children's stories with
"such unmalleable material as the somber, stern, and rigid Puritans," noting that Hawthorne consistently viewed his Puritan ancestors as "gloomy, joyless, and rigid."[6] Apparently, Hawthorne's
view of the Puritans distorted his picture of the past. As Hyatt
H. Waggoner puts it:

> Despite his long absorption in Puritan writings, it is
> pretty clear that Hawthorne had a typical nineteenth-
> century view of his ancestors. He exaggerated their
> gloominess and their intolerance and probably attributed
> their persecution of sexual offenses to ideas other than
> those they actually held.[7]

[4]"The Hawthorne Myth: A Protest," Essays and Studies by Members of the English Association, 16 (1963), 29-30.

[5]"The Genius of Nathaniel Hawthorne," North American Review,
129, No. 274 (Sept. 1879), 206.

[6]"Three Aspects of Hawthorne's Puritanism," New England
Quarterly, 36 (1963), 202.

[7]Hawthorne, A Critical Study (Cambridge: Harvard University
Press, 1963), p. 14.

SAMPLE PAPER: HAWTHORNE'S PURITANS   *119*

As A. N. Kaul says, "This archaism appears to have been a necessary condition for the richest engagement of his imagination, and
also, paradoxically, for his deepest intuitions of the modern
spirit."[8]

But we must concede that Hawthorne follows historical facts
at least part of the way. As he states in Chapter 2, the Puritans
were "a people amongst whom religion and law were almost identical." Page Smith reports that the early Puritans were forced to
confess their sins to the congregation, which consisted of almost
the entire population of the town. The penitent sinner was then
accepted back into the congregation, but the impenitent sinner
was excommunicated, regardless of the relative mildness of his
sin.[9] Hester, as Baughman points out, refuses to repent, and to
name her partner, and is thus isolated from the community (p. 544).

This tradition of public confession was continued later in
larger Puritan towns. Cases involving morals and religious beliefs were tried in civil courts and also punished by the church.[10]
The Scarlet Letter takes place in Boston, and apparently at such
a later date, with civil and religious authority collaborating,
and yet Hawthorne clearly dates his events in very early Puritan
times. The action occurs, he says, "not less than two centuries
ago" (Ch.2), that is, at some time before 1650, since The Scarlet

[8]Introduction, Hawthorne: A Collection of Critical Essays
(Englewood Cliffs: Prentice-Hall, 1966), p. 2.

[9]As a City upon a Hill (New York: Alfred A. Knopf, 1966),
pp. 60-61.

[10]Smith, pp. 129-130.

Letter was published in 1850. Hawthorne mentions that Hester has been sentenced by the magistrates. But when she is forced to stand on the scaffold, a civil punishment, the church, in the persons of the clergymen Wilson and Dimmesdale, urges her to reveal the name of her partner in sin. Years later, when Hester and Pearl visit the governor, he discusses the case with the Reverend Mr. Dimmesdale.

Not only civil and religious authorities were involved in the punishment of sin, but the people themselves. The townspeople are present at Hester's punishment. They avoid her when they meet her in public, and they tell their children stories about her. The punishments of standing on the scaffold and wearing the scarlet letter are effective only because they make Hester aware of the way the townspeople feel about her. Facing the stares of the people, on the scaffold and for years afterward, is her real punishment.

Beyond this union of church authority, state authority, and public opinion in the punishment of sin, Hester's treatment is not characteristic of Puritan justice and mercy. The scaffold itself, and Hester's being forced to stand on it for public scorn, are probably not historically accurate. In the early Puritan community, the sinner was usually punished only mildly, if at all, and was forgiven and reunited with the community after a public confession. Later, sinners were punished more severely, but the punishment was usually brief, such as an afternoon in the stocks or a whipping. Long-term punishments, such as jail sen-

tences, were almost nonexistent.[11] Some cases are recorded of
women being branded or forced to wear the letter "A," but such
cases were rare, and, according to Curtis P. Nettels, concerned
only habitual offenses:

> In seventeenth-century New England, women guilty of repeated
> moral lapses were whipped or occasionally forced to wear the
> scarlet letter; after 1720, whipping was resorted to only
> for serious offenders.[12]

Hester's offense is clearly not habitual: Hawthorne presents her
only arrest, and she has offended with one man only. Hawthorne's
townswomen who call for branding, and even death, are evidently
not authentic, as Hawthorne claims them to be: ". . . there was
a coarser fiber in those wives and maidens of old English birth
and breeding, than in their fair descendants . . . ." (Ch. 2).

Puritan religious and civil law covered such a wide range of
sins that everyone must have committed some sin at one time or
another, and, in fact, in some towns, nearly every citizen was
brought before the court during the course of a few years. Court
records are full of cases in which a man and a woman were forbid-
den to see each other or a woman was awarded payment from the
father of an illegitimate child.[13] Since these cases were public
knowledge, the sinner knew that he was not alone.

[11]Henry W. Lawrence, The Not-Quite Puritans (Boston: Little,
Brown, and Co., 1928), p. 171.

[12]The Roots of American Civilization: A History of American
Colonial Life, 2nd ed. (New York: Appleton-Century-Crofts, 1963),
p. 463.

[13]Edmund S. Morgan, "The Puritans and Sex," in Pivotal Interpretations of American History, ed. Carl N. Degler (New York:
Harper and Row, 1966), I, 11, 14.

The members of the early Puritan community were bound to forgive the penitent sinner and restore him to their community. Even when a member was excommunicated, he automatically became a member again if he confessed his guilt.[14] Baughman points out that the English Puritan societies practiced public confession, and naturally imported it to America when they came. Public confessions were required by the church and state in the Massachusetts Bay Colony from its beginning, and in Plymouth from 1624. John Winthrop's journal, with which Hawthorne was familiar, describes sixteen cases of public confession between 1630 and 1650, four of them for adultery.[15] In Groton, Massachusetts, sixty-six of the two hundred persons who were members of the town by baptismal covenant between 1761 and 1775 confessed to fornication before marriage. Nine of the sixteen couples admitted to full communion between 1789 and 1791 had confessed to fornication.[16]

The Puritans felt that the entire community was united in a covenant with God. The sins of one person could bring God's judgment on all. Therefore, for the common good, the community tried to redeem all sinners as quickly as possible and reunite them with the community.[17] Confession and punishment were forms of cleansing after which the sinner could rejoin the community,

[14]Smith, pp. 60-61.

[15]Baughman, pp. 533, 539.

[16]Smith, p. 62.

[17]Smith, pp. 7-8.

both religiously and socially, on an equal level with everyone
else and with no stigma. When one member of the community was
purged of sin and forgiven, the community was reunited, as a
child is reunited with his parents after being spanked.

Hester's permanent alienation from the community, though
partially self-imposed, is not characteristic of the Puritans.
Her punishment must be seen not as an example of the way the Puritans dealt with sinners, but as an example of an individual's
failure to accept the moral and legal system designed to reunite
him with the community, and of the community's failure to forgive
a sinner and restore him to full fellowship, under God's covenant. Hawthorne has freely interpreted Puritan beliefs about the
community, and about sin as isolating the individual and harming
the community.

Hester's public admission of her act, whether or not she
considered it sinful, and her punishment cleanse her of guilt,
just as they would have in historical times, but only if she had
fully confessed and repented. But Hester does not name her partner, and she remains impenitent and even, at first, defiant. She
refuses to accept the moral and legal system for reuniting the
sinner with the community; then she works out her own way,
through her needlecraft and care of the sick, to rejoin the community while still remaining isolated and independent.

Hawthorne does not present Hester as a case of Puritan injustice, as the beginning of his story suggests. Hester's story
presents not the injustice of the Puritan code, but a specific
instance wherein the code fails to preserve justice. Hawthorne

imagines a unique personality and a unique experience within the general context of Puritan beliefs. He creates not Puritan history, but what Kaul refers to as "the interpretative Puritan myth" (p. 9).

Dimmesdale and Chillingworth are similarly interpretative projections of Puritan beliefs, rather than authentic types. When one person broke the community's covenant with God by sinning, and was cast out for not repenting, the community was not whole. The sin spread throughout the community, as its members were tempted to hate or ignore the outcast, to gossip and act hypocritically. Smith gives the historical context:

> The congregations were doubtless on occasion cruel, and the system itself put fearful strains on the delinquent saints as well as their judges. But the records are impressive evidence of the fidelity with which most congregations observed scriptural injunctions to charity. Within a harsh system, they frequently showed great patience and forbearance with the sinners who appeared before them. If their church was a community of justice, it was also a community of mercy, surrogate for a Christ who had spoken of God's forgiveness as inexhaustible. (p. 63)

Smith further reports that the Puritans had "a country realism about sex that is in sharp contrast to late nineteenth-century sexual attitudes," which have pictured the Puritans inaccurately "as full of inhibitions, prudery, and repressions" (loc. cit.). The small Puritan town contained a great deal of illicit sex, most of it eventually confessed in public, repented, and accepted by the community as the usual human weakness. The Puritan community aimed chiefly to bring the lost soul back into fellowship with the community and with God, and to repair the break in their communal covenant.

Chillingworth is, of course, not a Puritan. But Hawthorne presents him as a kind of obsessive Puritan, in nineteenth-century terms, ruined by his inability to forgive sin, as an actual Puritan would have done. His psychological torture of Hester and Dimmesdale leads not to their reunion with society but to their further alienation. Dimmesdale lives a tortured life, unable to experience the purging from sin by confession and punishment that would reunite him psychologically with the community. His inhibitions and conscience, which shut him off from the Puritan system, probably belong, as Green would claim, to the nineteenth century rather than the seventeenth.

Hawthorne, in fact, has not created a historically accurate story. From the general Puritan beliefs about the wholeness of the community and the isolation of sin, he has projected three unique and atypical individuals. Through them, he works out his universal themes of alienation and social community, of sin, guilt, confession, punishment, and redemption. He has combined aspects of Puritan America with aspects of nineteenth-century America to create a story that is universal and symbolic, rather than historical. The story's only flaw lies in Hawthorne's misleading his readers to believe that his Puritans are historically authentic, as perhaps he himself mistakenly believed them to be.

BIBLIOGRAPHY

Baughman, Ernest W. "Public Confession and The Scarlet Letter," The New England Quarterly, 40 (1967), 532-550.

Cowley, Malcolm. The Portable Hawthorne, ed., with Introduction and Notes. New York: Viking Press, 1948.

Green, Martin. "The Hawthorne Myth: A Protest," Essays and Studies by Members of the English Association, 16 (1963), 16-36.

Kaul, A. N. Introduction, Hawthorne: A Collection of Critical Essays. Englewood Cliffs: Prentice-Hall, 1966.

Lawrence, Henry W. The Not-Quite Puritans. Boston: Little, Brown, and Co., 1928.

Levin, David. "Nathaniel Hawthorne, The Scarlet Letter," in The American Novel from James Fenimore Cooper to William Faulkner, ed. Wallace Stegner. New York: Basic Books, 1965. Pp. 13-24.

Morgan, Edmund S. "The Puritans and Sex," in Pivotal Interpretations of American History, ed. Carl N. Degler. New York: Harper and Row, 1966. I, 4-16.

Nettels, Curtis P. The Roots of American Civilization: A History of American Colonial Life. Second ed. New York: Appleton-Century-Crofts, 1963.

SAMPLE PAPER: HAWTHORNE'S PURITANS   *127*

Smith, Page. _As a City upon a Hill_. New York: Alfred A. Knopf,

    1966.

Schwartz, Joseph. "Three Aspects of Hawthorne's Puritanism,"

    New England Quarterly, 36 (1963), 192-208.

Trollope, Anthony. "The Genius of Nathaniel Hawthorne," _The_

    North American Review, 129, No. 274 (Sept. 1879), 203-223.

Waggoner, Hyatt H. _Hawthorne: A Critical Study_. Cambridge: Har-

    vard University Press, 1963.

Exercises

1. Select some well-known literary work: _Walden, David Copperfield, Huckleberry Finn, Alice in Wonderland, The Wind in the Willows, A Farewell to Arms._ Describe how thoroughly it is cataloged by your library. Check cards for author, title, and subject. How many editions does your library have? Is the work contained within any _Works?_ How many cards treat it as a subject? Does your library own a first edition? This last may require that you find the date of the first edition by looking up your author in an encyclopedia, checking available books about him, and perhaps checking in the British Museum's _General Catalogue of Printed Books_, or, for a twentieth-century book, _United States Catalog of Printed Books_ or _Cumulative Book Index_ to discover the earliest cataloging.

2. Choose a subject—"Dog Racing," "Vietnam," "Bowling," "Mushrooms," or what not—and write a short statistical report on the listings under this subject in the _Reader's Guide to Periodical Literature_ over the past ten years. Does your subject have unusually fat or lean years? What kinds of magazines treat the subject? Can you infer anything from your data about

fashions in magazines, or happenings in the world? Go to one article in the most prolific year to discover the reason for your subject's popularity.

3. Look up some event of the recent past (after 1913) in *The New York Times Index*. Write a paper on how the event is reported in the *Times* and in the other newspapers available in your library.

4. Write a brief description of two specialized indexes—for example, the *Art Index*, the *Dramatic Index*, the *Essay and General Literature Index*, the *Music Index*—telling what kinds of things you can learn from each, what kinds of things you would like to learn but cannot, and how convenient and informative each seems to be.

5. Selecting any well-known author, English or American (but avoid such giants as Shakespeare and Milton), go to the "Annual Bibliography" in *PMLA* for any year, and copy out the year's crop of articles on your man. Now go to an appropriate specialized bibliography for the same year —the one in the *Philological Quarterly*, for instance, or in *Modern Philology* or in *American Literature*—and write a report comparing the differing treatments of the two.

Suggested Subjects for Research Papers

A Famous Trial (Alger Hiss, Angela Davis, Daniel Ellsberg)

Abortion Laws: The Moral and Legal Issues

Symbolism in Faulkner's *The Bear* (Beckett's *Waiting for Godot*, Fellini's *8½*)

The Environment (Air or Water Pollution, Nuclear Power, Preservation of Species)

Drug Control: Pro or Con

An Issue in Women's Rights

Malcolm X

Ethnic Liberation Movements (Black, Chicano, American Indian)

Symbolism in Three Poems by Robert Frost (Robert Lowell, James Dickey)

The Urban Crisis

Censorship

Legislation to Control Guns

Why Johnny Can't Read

Pacifism and Violence

The Spiritual Revival (Zen, Jesus People, Buddhists, Fundamentalists)

Our Disappearing Whales (Wild Mustangs, Eagles)

New Life in Art (Happenings, Neorealism, Environmental Art)

APPENDIX A
A Writer's Grammar

You have now seen many of the ills of writing—the ailing thesis that weakens the whole system, the *of*-and-*which* disease, the recurring rash of wordiness. But many of your sentences may still suffer from ailments more deeply genetic. You can probably tell when a sentence feels bad, especially after your instructor has marked it up. You can, in other words, detect the symptoms, but to work an efficient cure you need also some skill in the old household remedies of grammar.

The Basic Parts of Speech

The parts of speech are the sentence's vital organs. Knowing the basic eight—nouns, pronouns, verbs, adjectives, adverbs, prepositions, conjunctions, and interjections—helps us control its midnight fevers.

Nouns. These name something. A *proper noun* names a particular person, place, or thing. A *common noun* names a general class of things; a common noun naming a group as a single unit is a *collective noun*. A phrase or clause functioning as a noun is a *noun phrase* or a *noun clause*. Here are some examples:

> *Common:* stone, tree, house, girl, artist, nation, democracy
> *Proper:* George, Miami, Europe, Declaration of Independence
> *Collective:* committee, family, quartet, herd, navy, clergy, kind
> *Noun phrase: Riding the surf* takes stamina.
> *Noun clause: What you say* may depend on *how you say it.*

Pronouns. As their name indicates, pronouns stand "for nouns." The noun a pronoun represents is called its *antecedent*. Pronouns may be classified as follows:

> *Personal (standing for persons):* I, you, he, she, we, they; me, him, her, us, them; my, his, our, and so on.
> *Reflexive (turning the action back on the doer):* I hurt *myself.* They enjoy *themselves.*

Intensive (*emphasizing the doer*): He *himself* said so.
Relative (*linking subordinate clauses*): who, which, that, whose, whomever, whichever, and so on.
Interrogative (*beginning a question*): who, which, what.
Demonstrative (*pointing to things*): this, that, these, those, such.
Indefinite (*standing for indefinite numbers of persons or things*): one, any, each, few, some, anyone, everyone, somebody, and so on.
Reciprocal (*plural reflexives*): each other, one another.

Verbs.   These express actions or states of being. A verb may be *transitive*, requiring an object to complete the thought, or *intransitive*, requiring no object for completeness. Some verbs can function either transitively or intransitively. *Linking verbs* link the subject to a state of being.

Transitive: He *put* his feet on the chair. She *hit* the ceiling. They *sang* a sad old song.
Intransitive: He *smiled*. She *cried*. They *sang* like birds.
Linking: He *is* happy. She *feels* angry. This *looks* bad.

Adjectives.   These describe nouns or pronouns. An *adjectival phrase* or *adjectival clause* functions in a sentence as a single adjective would.

Adjectives: The *green* house faces west. He was a *handsome* devil. The *old haunted* house was *empty*.
Adjectival phrase: He had reached the end *of the book*.
Adjectival clause: Here is the key *that unlocks the barn*.

Adverbs.   These describe verbs, adjectives, or other adverbs. An *adverbial phrase* or *adverbial clause* functions as a single adverb would.

Adverbs: Though *slightly* fat, he runs *quickly* and plays *extremely* well.
Adverbial phrase: He left *after the others*.
Adverbial clause: She lost the gloves *after she left the store*.

Prepositions.   A preposition links a noun or pronoun to another word in the sentence. A preposition and its object form a *prepositional phrase*.

By late afternoon, Williams was exhausted.
He walked *to* his car and drove *from* the field.

Conjunctions.   These join words, phrases, and clauses. Coordinating conjunctions—*and, but, or, yet, for*—join equals:

Mary *and* I won easily.

Near the shore *but* far from home, the bottle floated.
He was talented, *yet* he failed.

Subordinating conjunctions join minor thoughts to main ones:

Since it was late, they left.
He worked hard *because* he needed the grade.
They stopped *after* they reached the spring.

Interjections.   These interrupt the usual flow of the sentence to emphasize feelings:

But, *oh*, the difference to me.
Mr. Dowd, *alas*, has ignored the evidence.
The consumer will suddenly discover that, *ouch*, his dollar is cut in half.

These are the parts: now for some problems in how they work.

Agreement

Make your verb and its subject agree.

Match singulars with singulars, plurals with plurals. First find the verb, since that names the action—*sways* in the following sentence: "The poplar tree sways in the wind, dropping yellow leaves on the lawn." Then ask *who* or *what* sways, and you have your simple subject: *tree*, a singular noun. Then make sure that your singular subject matches its singular verb. You will have little trouble except when subject and verb are far apart, or when the number of the subject itself is doubtful. (Is *family* singular or plural? What about *none?* What about *neither he nor she?*)

Faulty: *Revision* of their views about markets and averages *are* mandatory.
Revised: Revision of their views about markets and averages *is* mandatory.

Sidestep the plural constructions that fall between your singular subject and its verb:

Faulty: The *attention* of the students *wander* out the window.
Revised: The *attention* of the students *wanders* out the window.

Faulty: The *plaster*, as well as the floors, *need* repair.
Revised: The *plaster*, as well as the floors, *needs* repair.

Collective nouns (*committee, jury, herd, group, family, kind, quartet*) are single units; give them singular verbs, or plural members:

Faulty: Her *family were* ready.
Revised: Her *family was* ready.

Faulty: The *jury have disagreed* among themselves.
Revised: The *jurors have disagreed* among themselves.

Faulty: These *kind* of muffins *are* delicious.
Revised: These muffins are delicious.
Revised: This kind of muffin *is* delicious.

Watch out for the indefinite pronouns—*each, neither, anyone, everyone, no one, none, everybody, nobody.* Each of these is (not *are*) singular in idea, yet each flirts with the crowd from which it singles out its idea: each of *these,* either of *them,* none of *them.* Give all of them singular verbs.

None of these men *is* a failure.
None of the class, even the best prepared, *wants* the test.
Everybody, including the high-school kids, *goes* to Andy's Drive-In.
Neither the right nor the left *supports* the issue.

Exception: when one side, or both, of the either-or contrast is plural, the verb is plural:

Either the players or the coach *are* bad.
Neither the rights of man nor the needs of the commonwealth *are* relevant to the question.

Don't let a plural noun in the predicate lure you into a plural verb:

Faulty: His most faithful rooting *section are* his family and his girl.
Revised: His most faithful rooting *section is* his family and his girl.

Aligning the Verbs

Verbs have *tense* (past, present, future), *mood* (indicative, imperative, subjunctive), and *voice* (active, passive). These can sometimes slip out of line, as your thought slips.

Keep your tenses in mind.

Your thoughts can slip from present to past, especially when describing events in literature, which you should *put in the present tense,* to reflect their timeless presence. (Hamlet will still be hesitating, timelessly and forever, when you and I are dead.) But because your experience of reading always comes before you write about it, and because novels and stories are told in the past tense (*he said, she said*), your mind will frequently slip into the past as you describe the events in a literary work, even though you have started properly in the present:

> *Faulty:* Hamlet *finds* the king praying, but he *was* unable to act, and he *let* his best opportunity slip.
>
> *Revised:* Hamlet *finds* the king praying, but he *is* unable to act, and he *lets* his best opportunity slip.

Set your tense, then move your reader clearly forward or back from it as your thought requires:

> Hamlet *finds* the king praying. He *had sworn* instant revenge the night before, but he *will achieve* it only by accident and about a week later. Here he *is* unable to act; he *loses* his best opportunity.

Keep your moods in mind.

The *indicative mood,* which indicates matters of fact (our usual verb and way of writing), and the *imperative mood,* which commands ("Do this," "Keep your moods in mind"), will give you no trouble. The *subjunctive mood,* which expresses an action or condition not asserted as actual fact, occasionally will. The conditional, provisional, wishful, suppositional ideas expressed by the subjunctive are usually subjoined (*subjunctus,* "yoked under") in subordinate clauses. The form of the verb is often plural, even though the subject is singular.

> He looked as if he *were* confident.
> If I *were* you, Miles, I would ask her myself.
> If this *be* error, and upon me [*be*] proved . . . .
> *Had* he *been* sure, he would have said so.
> I demand that he *make* restitution.
> I move that the nominations *be closed,* and that the secretary *cast* a unanimous ballot.

Avoid awkward or faulty shifts of mood:

> *Faulty:* If I *was* you, John, I would speak for myself.
> *Revised:* If I *were* you, John, I would speak for myself.

> *Faulty:* If he *would have known,* he never would have said that.
> *Revised:* If he *had known,* he never would have said that.
> *Revised: Had* he *known,* he never would have said that.

Faulty: He moved that the club buy the picture, and that the secretary *shall bill* the members.

Revised: He moved that the club buy the picture, and that the secretary *bill* the members.

Faulty: You *should read* carefully and *don't miss* his irony.

Revised: You *should read* carefully *to avoid missing* his irony.

Revised: *Read* carefully, and *don't miss* his irony.

Don't mix active and passive voice.

One parting shot at our friend the passive. If you can eradicate it from your habits altogether, you can avoid, as we have seen, all misalignments of active with passive in the same sentence:

As he *entered* the room, voices *were heard* [he *heard*].

After they *laid out* the pattern, electric shears *were used* [they *used* electric shears].

You can also think of this as an awkward shift of subject, from *he* to *voices*, from *they* to *shears*. Here is a slippery sample, where the subject stays the same:

Faulty: This plan *reduces* taxes and *has been proved* workable in three other cities.

Revised: This plan *reduces* taxes and *has proved* workable in three other cities.

Revised: This plan, proved workable in three other cities, reduces taxes.

Practice A

Straighten out these disagreements and misalignments.

1. None of us are perfect.
2. These kind of questions are sheer absurdities.
3. Conservatism, as well as liberalism, are summonses for change in American life as we know it.
4. The entire electorate are do-gooders or do-nothings.
5. Neither the fringe on his jacket nor the price of his guitar impress us.
6. Her family were bitter about it.
7. The grazing ground of both the antelope and the wild horses are west of this range.
8. The campus, as well as the town, need to wake up.
9. The extinction of several species of whales are threatened.
10. None of the group, even Smith and Jones, want to play.

11. Holden goes to New York. He looked up his old teacher and called his old girl friend. Before he started, he had decided to call his sister, but actually he took almost the whole book to get around to calling her. In the end, she proved to be his best friend.
12. If I would have studied harder, I would have passed.
13. They insisted that he shows up.
14. The sit-in accomplished its purpose and was tested by fire.
15. First he investigated the practical implications, and then the moral implications that were involved were examined.

Reference of Pronouns

Match your pronouns to what they stand for.

Pronouns stand for (*pro*) nouns. They *refer* back to nouns already expressed (*antecedents*), or they stand for conceptions (people, things, ideas) already established or implied, as in "*None* of *them* is perfect." Pronouns must agree with the singular and plural ideas they represent.

When a relative pronoun (*who, which, that*) is the subject of a clause, it takes a singular verb if its antecedent is singular, a plural verb if its antecedent is plural:

Phil is the only *one* of our swimmers WHO *has* won three gold medals.
[The antecedent is *one*, not *swimmers*.]
Phil is one of the best *swimmers* WHO *have* ever been on the team.
[The antecedent is *swimmers*, not *one*.]

Pronouns may stand either as subjects or objects of the action, and their form changes accordingly.

Use subjective pronouns for subjective functions.

Those pronouns in the predicate that refer back to the subject are troublesome; keep them subjective:

This is *he*.
He discovered that it was *I*.
It was *they* who signed the treaty.

Another example is that of the pronoun in *apposition* with the subject (that is, *positioned near,* and meaning the same thing as, the subject):

We students would rather talk than sleep.

After *than* and *as,* the pronoun is usually the subject of an implied verb:

She is taller than *I* [am].
You are as bright as *he* [is].
She loves you as much as *I* [love you].

But note: "She loves you as much as [she loves] *me.*" Match your pronouns to what they stand for, subjects for subjects, objects for objects.

Use a subjective pronoun as subject of a noun clause. This is the trickiest of pronominal problems, because the subject of the clause also looks like the object of the main verb:

Faulty: The sergeant asked *whomever* did it to step forward.
Revised: The sergeant asked *whoever* did it to step forward.

Similarly, parenthetical remarks like *I think, he says,* and *we believe* often make pronouns seem objects when they are actually subjects:

Faulty: Ellen is the girl *whom* I think *will succeed.*
Revised: Ellen is the girl *who* I think *will succeed.*

Use objective pronouns for objective functions.

Compound objects give most of the trouble. Try the pronoun by itself: "complimented *me,*" "sent *him,*" and so forth. These are all correct:

The mayor complimented Bill and *me.*
Between *her* and *me,* an understanding grew.
They sent it to Stuart and *him.*
. . . for you and *me.*
He would not think of letting *us* girls help him.

Use a possessive pronoun before a gerund.

Gerunds are *-ing* words used as nouns, so the pronouns attached to them must say what they mean:

Faulty: She disliked *him* hunting.
Revised: She disliked *his* hunting.

The object of her dislike is not *him* but *hunting.*

Keep your antecedents clear.

If an antecedent is missing, ambiguous, vague, or remote, the pronoun will suffer from "faulty reference."

> *Missing:* In Texas *they* produce a lot of oil.
> *Revised:* Texas produces a lot of oil.
>
> *Ambiguous:* Paul smashed into a girl's car *who* was visiting his sister.
> *Revised:* Paul smashed into the car of a *girl* visiting his sister.
>
> *Vague:* Because Ann had never spoken before an audience, she was afraid of *it.*
> *Revised:* Because Ann had never spoken before an audience, she was afraid.
>
> *Remote:* The castle was built in 1537. The rooms and furnishings are carefully kept up, but the entrance is now guarded by a coin-fed turnstile. *It* still belongs to the Earl.
> *Revised:* The castle, which still belongs to the Earl, was built in 1537. The rooms and furnishings are carefully kept up, but the entrance is now guarded by a coin-fed turnstile.

This poses a special problem, especially when heading a sentence ("This is a special problem"). Many good stylists insist that every *this* refer back to a specific noun—*report* in the following example:

> The commission submitted its *report. This* proved windy, evasive, and ineffectual.

Others occasionally allow (as I do) a more colloquial *this,* referring back more broadly:

> The commission submitted its report. This ended the matter.

This broad *this* gets by nicely (I hope), even though the *submission,* to which it refers, does not specifically appear, so named, and even though it could refer, ambiguously, to *report.* The rule here would seem to be: clear up all risky ambiguities, and avoid sinning.

> *Ambiguous:* The commission submitted its report. This was wholly ineffectual.
> *Revised:* The commission submitted its report, a wholly ineffectual gesture.

Give an indefinite or general antecedent a singular pronoun.

> *Faulty:* Modern suburban *woman* is often more interested in *their* social standing than in *their* children.
> *Revised:* Modern suburban *woman* is often more interested in *her* social standing than in *her* children.

Faulty: **Each** of the students hoped to follow *their* teacher's footsteps.

Revised: Each of the students hoped to follow *the* teacher's footsteps.

Faulty: If the *clergy* dares to face the new philosophy, *they* should declare *themselves*.

Revised: If the *clergy* dares to face the new philosophy, the *clergy* should declare *itself*.

Keep person and number consistent.

Don't slip from person to person (*I* to *they*); don't fall among singulars and plurals—or you will get bad references.

Faulty: **They** have reached an age when *you* should know better.

Revised: **They** have reached an age when *they* should know better.

Faulty: A motion *picture* can improve upon a book, but *they* usually do not.

Revised: A motion *picture* can improve upon a book, but *it* usually does not.

Practice B

Revise these faulty pronouns, and their sentences where necessary.

1. None of us are perfect.
2. Doug is the only one of the boys who always stand straight.
3. We are stronger than them.
4. They elected Mary and I vice-president and president respectively.
5. Jim will vote for whomever they say is a winner.
6. He opened the bird's cage, and it flew away.
7. It was him all right.
8. She disliked him whistling the same old tune.
9. He will give the ticket to whomever wants it: he did it for you and I.
10. My mother insists on me buying my own clothes: the average girl likes their independence.
11. The buffalo is far from extinct. Their numbers are actually increasing.
12. The program was turned into a fiasco by bad planning. This was bad.

Modifiers Misused and Misplaced

Keep your adjectives and adverbs straight.

The adjective sometimes wrongly crowds out the adverb: "He played a *real* conservative game." And the adverb sometimes steals the adjective's place, especially when the linking verb looks transitive but isn't (*feels, looks, tastes, smells*), making the sense wrong: "He feels *badly*" (adverb) means incompetence, not misery. Similarly, certain adjectives ending in -ly (*lonely, lovely, leisurely*) tend to masquerade as adverbs: "She swam *lovely*," "He walked *leisurely*." The cure is in modifying your nouns with adjectives, and modifying everything else with adverbs:

> He played a *really* conservative game. [adverb]
> He feels *bad*. [adjective]
> She swam *beautifully*. [adverb]
> He walked *slowly*. [adverb]

Some words serve both as adjectives and adverbs: *early, late, near, far, only, little, right, wrong, straight, well, better, best, fast,* for example. These words are linguistic windfalls, to be squeezed for their juice:

> Think *little* of *little* things.

Near is a hard case, serving as an adjective (*the near future*) and as an adverb of place (*near the barn*), and then also trying to serve for *nearly,* the adverb of degree.

> *Faulty:* We are nowhere *near* knowledgeable enough.
> *Revised:* We are not *nearly* knowledgeable enough.

> *Faulty:* It was a *near* treasonous statement.
> *Revised:* It was a *nearly* treasonous statement.

> *Faulty:* With Dodge, he has a tie of *near*-filial rapport.
> *Revised:* With Dodge, he has an *almost* filial rapport.

Slow has a long history as an adverb, but *slowly* keeps the upper hand in print. Notice that adverbs usually go after, and adjectives before:

> The *slow* freight went *slowly*.

Make your comparisons complete.

Ask yourself "Than what?"—when you find your sentences ending with a *greener* (adjective) or a *more smoothly* (adverb):

> *Faulty:* The western plains are *flatter*.
> *Revised:* The western plains are *flatter than* those east of the Mississippi.

Faulty: He plays more *skillfully.*
Revised: He plays more *skillfully than* most boys his age.

Faulty: Jane told her more than Ellen.
Revised: Jane told her more than she told Ellen.

Faulty: His income is lower than a *busboy.*
Revised: His income is lower than a *busboy's.*
Revised: His income is lower than that of a busboy.

Don't let your modifiers squint.

Some modifiers squint in two directions at once. Place them to modify one thing only.

Faulty: They agreed *when both sides ceased fire* to open negotiations.
Revised: They agreed to open negotiations *when both sides ceased fire.*

Faulty: Several delegations *we know* have failed.
Revised: *We know* that several delegations have failed.

Faulty: They hoped to try *thoroughly* to understand.
Revised: They hoped to try to understand *thoroughly.*

Faulty: He resolved to dependably develop plans.
Revised: He resolved to develop dependable plans.

Don't let your modifiers or references dangle.

The *-ing* words (the gerunds and participles) tend to slip loose from the sentence and dangle, referring to nothing or the wrong thing.

Faulty: Going home, the walk was slippery. [participle]
Revised: Going home, I found the walk slippery.

Faulty: When getting out of bed, his toe hit the dresser. [gerund]
Revised: When getting out of bed, he hit his toe on the dresser.

Infinitive phrases also can dangle badly:

Faulty: To think clearly, some logic is important.
Revised: To think clearly, you should learn some logic.

Any phrase or clause may dangle:

Faulty: When only a freshman [phrase], Jim's history teacher inspired him.

Revised: When Jim was only a freshman, his history teacher inspired him.

Faulty: After he had taught thirty years [clause], the average student still seemed average.

Revised: After he had taught thirty years, he found the average student still average.

Practice C

1. Straighten out these adjectives and adverbs:

The demonstration reached near riot proportions.
It smells awfully.
The dress fitted her perfect.
He has a reasonable good chance.
His car had a special built engine.

2. Complete and adjust these partial thoughts:

He swims more smoothly.
The pack of a paratrooper is lighter than a soldier.
The work of a student is more intense than his parents.
This is the best painting.
The moon is smaller.

3. Unsquint these modifiers:

She planned on the next day to call him.
They asked after ten days to be notified.
The party promised to completely attempt reform.
Several expeditions we know have failed.
We wanted to win enough to cry.

4. Mend these danglers:

What we need is a file of engineers broken down by their specialties.
Following the games on television, the batting average of every player was at his fingertips.
When entering the room, the lamp fell over.
To study well, a quiet room helps.
After he arrived at the dorm, his father phoned.

Fragments, Comma Splices, and Run-ons

Align your thoughts as complete sentences.

As you have seen, the fragment—any piece of a sentence, with subject or predicate missing—may have superb rhetorical force:

"So what." But when fragments slip in unnoticed, they reveal a failure to grasp the sentence completely. You have lost the fundamental connection between subject and verb, and the parts related to them.

> *Faulty:* He does not spell everything out. But rather hints that something is wrong, and leaves the rest up to the reader.
>
> *Revised:* He does not *spell* everything out, but rather *hints* . . . , and *leaves* . . . . [subject with compound verb, set off by commas]

> *Faulty:* Yet here is her husband treating their son to all that she considers evil. Plus the fact that the boy is offered beer.
>
> *Revised:* Yet here is her husband treating their son to all that she considers evil, especially beer.

> *Faulty:* He points out that one never knows what the future will bring. Because it is actually a matter of luck.
>
> *Revised:* He points out that one never knows what the future will bring, because it is actually a matter of luck. [dependent clause now properly connected]

With run-ons—two sentences shuffled together as one—the grammatical grip is even more feeble than with the fragment. Somehow the writer has never grasped the sentence as a discrete marriage of subject and verb. All kinds of parties just stumble in together:

> *Faulty:* He went to class, he forgot his paper. [comma splice]
>
> *Faulty:* He went to class he forgot his paper. [run-on sentence]
>
> *Revised:* (a) He went to class. He forgot his paper.
>
> (b) He went to class; he forgot his paper.
>
> (c) He went to class, but he forgot his paper.
>
> (d) When he got to class, he found that he had forgotten his paper.

Conjunctive adverbs (*however, therefore, nevertheless, moreover, furthermore,* and others) may cause trouble.

> *Faulty:* She bought the blouse, however her heart was not in it.
>
> *Revised:* (a) She bought the blouse, but her heart was not in it.
>
> (b) She bought the blouse; however, her heart was not in it.
>
> (c) She bought the blouse; her heart, however, was not in it.

Similarly, transitional phrases (*in fact, that is, for example*) may run your sentences together:

> *Faulty:* He disliked discipline, that is, he really was lazy.
>
> *Revised:* (a) He disliked discipline; that is, he really was lazy.
>
> (b) He disliked discipline, that is, anything demanding.

Practice D

1. Correct the following:

He left his second novel unfinished. Perhaps because of his basic uncertainty, which he never overcame.

He entered the race for the presidency. Knowing all along that he could not win.

He seems to play a careless game. But actually knows exactly what he is doing, and intends to put his opponent off guard.

He played to win, that is, he gave every game all he had.

His idea of democracy was incomplete he himself had slaves.

2. Cure the following grammatical ailments:

The professor, as well as the students, were glad the course was over.

They study hard at State, but you do not have to work all the time.

Holden goes to New York and learned about life.

As he looked up, a light could be seen in the window.

A citizen should support the government, but they should also be free to criticize it.

It will all come true, for you and I.

The students always elect whomever is popular.

She hated me leaving so early.

This is one of the best essays that has been submitted.

While playing the piano, the dog sat by me and howled.

The team had a near perfect record.

Run-on sentences show a failure deeper than fragments.

3. Rewrite a paragraph, or other selected improvable passages, from one of your earlier papers.

APPENDIX B
Spelling and Capitalization

Learn to spell the words you use.

Spelling will increase your vocabulary and your grasp of meanings, as you spell out the meaningful parts. But everyone misspells a few old favorites—until fed up with himself. The dictionary is your best friend, in the presence of these enemies, but three underlying principles and some tricks of the trade can help immeasurably.

Principle I. Letters represent sounds: proNUNciation can help you spell. No one proNOUNcing his words would make the familiar errors of *similar* and *environment*. You can even improve your social standing by learning to say *envIRONment* and *goverNment* and *FebRUary* and *intRAmural*. Simply sound out the letters. You can even say *convertIble* and *indelIible* and *plausIble* without sounding like a fool, and you can silently stress the *able* in words like *probABLE* and *immovABLE* to remember the difficult distinction between words ending in *-ible* and *-able*.

Consonants reliably represent their sounds. Remember that *c* and *g* go soft before *i* and *e*. Consequently you must add a *k* when extending words like *picnic* and *mimic—picnicKing, mimicKing*—to keep them from rhyming with *slicing* or *dicing*. Conversely, you just keep the *e* (where you would normally drop it) when making *peace* into *peacEable* and *change* into *changEable*.

Single *s* is pronounced *zh* in words like *vision, occasion, pleasure.* Knowing that *ss* hushes ("sh-h-h") will keep you from errors like *occassion*, which would sound like *passion*.

Vowels sound short and light before single consonants: *hat, pet, mit(t), hop, mut(t)*. When you add any vowel (including *y*), the first vowel will say its name: *hate, Pete, mite, hoping, mutable*. Notice how the *a* in *-able* keeps the main vowel saying its name in words like *unmistakable, likable,* and *notable*. Therefore, to keep a vowel short, protect it with a double consonant: *petting, hopping*. This explains the troublesome *rr* in *occuRRence*: a single *r* would make it say *cure* in the middle. *Putting* a golf ball and *putting* something on paper must both use *tt* to keep from being pronounced *pewting*. Compare *stony* with *sonny* and *bony* with *bonny*. The *y* is replacing the *e* in *stone* and *bone*, and the rule is working perfectly. It works in any accented syllable: compare *forgeTTable* as against *markeTing*, and *begiNNing* as against *buttoNing*, and *compeLLing* as against *traveLing*.

Likewise, when *full* combines and loses its stress, it also loses an *l*. Note the single and double *l* in *fulFILLment*. Similarly, *SOULful*, *GRATEful*, *AWful*—even *SPOONful*.

Principle II. This is the old rule of *i* before *e*, and its famous exception:

> **I before *e***
> **Except after *c*,**
> **Or when sounded like *a***
> **As in *neighbor* and *weigh*.**

It works like a charm (*achieve, believe; receive, conceive*). Note that *c* needs an *e* to make it sound like *s*. Remember also that *leisure* was once pronounced "lay-sure"; and *foreign*, "for-ayn." Memorize these important exceptions: *seize, weird, either, sheik, forfeit, counterfeit*. Note that all are pronounced "ee" (with a little crowding) and that the *e* comes first. Then note that another small group goes the opposite way, having a long *i* sound as in the German *Heil: height, sleight, seismograph, kaleidoscope*. *Financier*, another exception, follows its French origin and its original sound.

Principle III. Most big words, following the Latin or French from which they came, spell their sounds letter for letter. Look up the derivations of the words you misspell (note the double *s* in *misspell*, and explain it). You will never again have trouble with *desperate* and *separate*, once you discover that the first comes from *de-spero*, "without hope," and that se*PAR*ate divides equals, as the PAR values in stocks or golf, nor with *definite* or *definitive*, once you see the kinship of both with *finite* and *finish*. Derivations can also help you a little with the devilment of -*able* and -*ible*, since, except for a few ringers, the *i* remains from Latin, and the -*ables* are either French (*ami-able*), or Anglo-Saxon copies (*work-able*). Knowing origins can help at crucial points: *resemblAnce* comes from Latin *simulAre*, "to copy"; *existEnce* comes from Latin *existEre*, "to stand forth." Similarly, you can link your unaccented errors with their accented relatives: *hypocrIsy-hypocrIte, irritAble-irritAte*.

The biggest help comes from learning the common Latin prefixes, which by assimilation (*ad-similis*, "like to like") account for the double consonants at the first syLLabic joint of so many of our words. Pronunciation has made those two tongue-twisting consonants the same—*aD-Similis* has become *aSSimilate; syN-Labium* has become *syLLable; in-Lumen* has become *iLLuminate:*

AD- (toward, to): *abbreviate* (shorten down), *accept* (grasp to).

CON- (with): *collapse* (fall with), *commit* (send with).

DIS- (apart): *dissect* (cut apart), *dissolve* (loosen apart).

IN- (into): *illuminate* (shine into), *illusion* (playing into).

IN- (not): *illegal* (not lawful), *immature* (not ripe).

INTER- (between): *interrupt* (break between), *interrogate* (ask between).

OB- (towards, to): *occupy* (take in), *oppose* (put to), *offer* (carry to).

SUB- (under): *suffer* (bear under), *suppose* (put down).

SYN- (together—this one is Greek): *symmetry* (measuring together), *syllogism* (logic together).

Spelling takes a will, an eye, and an ear. And a dictionary. Keep a list of your favorite enemies. Memorize one or two a day. Write them in the air in longhand. Visualize them. Imagine a blinking neon sign, with the wicked letters red and tall—d e f i n I t e—d e f i n I t e. Then print them once, write them twice, and blink them a few times more as you go to sleep. But best of all, make up whatever devices you can—the crazier the better—to remember the tricky parts:

DANCE attenDANCE.

EXISTENCE is TENSE.

There's IRON in this enviRONment.

The resisTANCE took its STANCE.

There's an ANT on the defendANT.

LOOSE as a goose.

LOSE loses an o.

ALLOT isn't A LOT.

ALREADY isn't ALL RIGHT.

I for gaIety.

The LL in paraLLel gives me *el.*

PURr in PURsuit.

Here are some more of the perpetual headaches:

accept—except

accommodate

acknowledgment—judgment

advice—advise

affect—effect

allusion—illusion—disillusion

analysis—analyzing—annual

apologize—Apollo

arrangement—argument

businessman

capital—capitol

careful—successful—fulfillment

challenge

cite—site—insight

committee
complement—compliment
council—counsel—consul
curriculum—career—occurrence
decide—divide—devices
desert—dessert
despair—desperate—separate
detrimental—dealt
dilemma—condemn
disastrous
embarrassment
eminent—imminent—immanent
exaggerate
explanation

forward—foreword
genius—ingenious
height—eighth
hypocrisy—democracy
irritable
lonely—loneliness
Negroes—heroes—tomatoes
obstacle
operate—opus—opera
possession
primitive
principal—principle
proceed—precede—procedure
until—till

Check your capitals.

You know about sentences and names, certainly; but the following points are troublesome. Capitalize:

1. Names of races and languages—Negro, Indian, French, English.
2. North, south, east, and west ONLY WHEN THEY ARE REGIONS—the mysterious East, the new Southwest.
3. The COMPLETE names of churches, rivers, hotels, and the like—the First Baptist Church, the Mark Hopkins Hotel, the Suwannee River (not First Baptist church, Mark Hopkins hotel, Suwannee river).
4. All words in titles, except prepositions, articles, and conjunctions. But capitalize even these if they come first or last, or if they are longer than five letters—"I'm Through with Love," *Gone with the Wind,* "I'll Stand By," *In Darkest Africa.* Capitalize nouns, adjectives, and prefixes in hyphenated compounds—*The Eighteenth-Century Background, The Anti-Idealist* (but *The Anti-slavery Movement;* check your dictionary). With magazines and newspapers in sentences, drop the *The* as part of the title (the *Saturday Evening Post,* the *Kansas City Star*).
5. References to a specific section of a work—the Index, his Preface, Chapter I, Act II, Scene iii, Volume IV.
6. Abstract nouns, when you want emphasis, serious or humorous —". . . the truths contradict, so what is Truth?"; Very Important Person; the Ideal.

DO NOT capitalize the seasons—spring, winter, midsummer.

DO NOT capitalize after a colon, unless what follows is normally capitalized:

In the end, it was useless: Adams really was too green.
We remember Sherman's words: "War is hell."
All effort is painful: pleasure comes with achievement.
The committee considered three things: (1) how to reduce expenditures, (2) how to raise more money, and (3) how to handle Smith's unfortunate laxity.

Exercises

1. Make a list of your five most frequent misspellings. Then keep it handy and active, removing your conquests and adding your new troubles.

2. Capitalize the following, and italicize where necessary:

go west, young man.
the east side of town
east side, west side
the tall negro spoke french.
she loved the spring.
health within seconds (book)
the methodist episcopal
    church

the missouri river
the new york public library
the neo-positivistic approach
    (book)
the country gentleman
    (magazine)
the st. louis post-dispatch

APPENDIX C
A Glossary
of Usage

Speech keeps a daily pressure on writing, and writing returns the compliment, exacting sense from new twists in the spoken language and keeping old senses straight. Usage, generally, is "the way they say it." Usage is the current in the living stream of language; it keeps us afloat, it keeps us fresh—as it sweeps us along. But to distinguish himself the writer must always battle it, must always swim upstream. He may say, "Hooja-eatwith?"; but he will write: "With whom did they compare themselves? With the best, with whoever seemed admirable." Usage is, primarily, talk; and talk year by year gives words differing social approval, and differing meanings. Words move from the gutter to the penthouse, and back down the elevator shaft. *Bull*, a four-letter Anglo-Saxon word, was unmentionable in Victorian circles. One had to use *he-cow*, if at all. Phrases and syntactical patterns also have their fashions, mostly bad. *Like unto me* changes to *like me* to *like I do; this type of thing* becomes *this type thing; -wise*, after centuries of dormancy in only a few words (*likewise, clockwise, otherwise*), suddenly sprouts out the end of everything: *budgetwise, personalitywise, beautywise, prestigewise.* Suddenly, everyone is saying *hopefully.* As usual, the marketplace changes more than your money.

But the written language has always refined the language of the marketplace. The Attic Greek of Plato and Aristotle (as Aristotle's remarks about local usages show) was distilled from commercial exchange. Cicero and Catullus and Horace polished their currency against the archaic and the Greek. Mallarmé claimed that Poe had given *un sens plus pur aux mots de la tribu*—which Eliot rephrases for himself: "to purify the dialect of the tribe." It is the very nature of writing so to do; it is the writer's illusion that he has done so:

I have laboured to refine our language to grammatical purity, and to clear it from colloquial barbarisms, licentious idioms, and irregular combinations. Something, perhaps, I have added to the elegance of its construction, and something to the harmony of its cadence.

—wrote Samuel Johnson as he closed his *Rambler* papers. And he had almost done what he hoped. He was to shape English writing for the next hundred years, until it was ready for another dip in the stream and another purification. His work, moreover, lasts. We would not imitate it now; but we can read it with pleasure, and imitate its enduring drive for excellence.

Johnson goes on to say that he has "rarely admitted any word not authorized by former writers." Writers provide the second level of usage, the paper money. But even this usage requires principle. If we accept "what the best writers use," we still cannot tell whether it is sound: we may be aping their bad habits. John F. Kennedy's inaugural address, carefully polished by Harvard's best, contains this oddity (my italics): "For man holds in his mortal hands the power to abolish *all form* of human poverty and *all form* of human life."* Clearly, he meant either *all forms* or *every form*—or *all* human poverty and *all* human life. This mixing of choices, this coupling of the collective *all* with singular *form*, can mean only something like "all traces of form," as if the President were melting a statue. Most singular indeed! Even the best go wrong.

So we cannot depend on usage for our rules. Usage is only a court of first appeal, where we can say little more than "He said it." Beyond that helpless litigation, we can test our writing by reason, and by simple principles: clarity is good, economy is good, ease is good, gracefulness is good, fullness is good, forcefulness is good. As with all predicaments on earth, we judge by appeal to principles, and we often find principles in conflict. Is it economical but unclear? Is it full but cumbersome? Is it clear but too colloquial for grace? Careful judgment will give the ruling.

Which is right, "I feel *bad*" or "I feel *badly*"? "The dress looks *good* on her" or "The dress looks *well* on her"? The man on the street would say, "I feel *bad*" and "The dress looks *good*," and he would be right: not because of "usage," but because *badly* would indicate shaky fingers and *well* a dress with good eyes. "Tie it tight" means "Tie it so that it is tight." Unfortunately, people trying to be proper follow the pattern of "He writes badly" and fall into the errors of "I feel badly" and "Tie it tightly." But *writes badly* is a verb with an adverb telling how the

---

* As delivered, and as given in the official press release, Jan. 21, 1961 (*New York Herald Tribune*, Late City Edition, p. 1; *Chicago Daily Tribune*, p. 4). *Form* was corrected to *forms* by the *New York Times*, Jan. 21, 1961, p. 4, and was read as *forms* into the *Congressional Record*, Doc. No. 9, 87th Cong., 1st sess.

action is done, and *feel bad* is a verb with a predicate adjective modifying the subject and telling how the subject *is*. The predicate adjective describes existences, as in *ring true* and *come thick:* "they ring, and they are true"; "they come, and they are thick." So it is with other verbs pointing to states of being—*seem, appear, become, grow, sound, smell, taste*—on which "good usage" might rule the wrong way. Just remember that you don't say "I feel goodly." Let reason be your guide.

Likewise with *the reason . . . is because.* You can find this colloquial redundancy on many a distinguished page. But everything a good writer writes is not necessarily good. The phrase is a collision between two choices, as the mind rushes after its meaning: between (1) *the reason is that . . .* and (2) *it is . . . because.* Delete *the reason . . . is,* the colloquial pump primer, and you save three words, sometimes four (the following eminent sentence, in which I have bracketed the surplus words, also suffers some redundancy of the *be*'s):

> In general it may be said that [the reason why] scholasticism was held to be an obstacle to truth [was] because it seemed to discourage further inquiry along experimental lines.

And so, usage is perhaps where we begin; but if we end there, we may end in wordiness and mediocrity. Clarity and economy are better guides than mere usage. The following prescriptions are just about what the doctor ordered to keep you ticking, and in good company. They summarize the practices of the most careful writers—those who constantly attend to what words mean. They provide tips on avoiding wordiness, and avoiding those slips in diction that sometimes turn your reception a little chilly.

Practical Prescriptions for Good Writing

A, an.   Use *a* before *h* sounded in a first syllable: *a hospital, a hamburger.* Use *an* before a silent *h: an honor, an heir, an hour.*

Above.   For naturalness and effectiveness, avoid such references as "The above statistics are . . . ," and "The above speaks for itself." Simply use "These" or "This."

Aesthetic.   An adjective: *an aesthetic judgment, his aesthetic viewpoint. Aesthetics* is singular for the science of beauty: "Santayana's *aesthetics* agrees with his metaphysics."

Affect. *Affect* means "to produce an *effect.*" Don't use it as a noun; just say *feeling* or *emotion*. *Affective* is a technical term for *emotional* or *emotive*, which are clearer.

Aggravate. Means to add gravity to something already bad enough. Avoid using it to mean "irritate."

WRONG	RIGHT
He aggravated his mother.	The rum aggravated his mother's fever.

All ready, already. Two different meanings. *All ready* means that everything is ready; *already* means "by this time."

All right, alright. *Alright* is not all right; you are confusing it with the spelling of *already*.

Alot. You mean *a lot*, not *allot*.

Also. Do not use for *and*, especially to start a sentence; not "*Also*, it failed," but simply "And it failed."

And/or. An ungainly hair splitter and thought stopper. You never *say* it. Don't write "for stage and/or screen"; write "for stage or screen, or both."

Ante-, anti. *Ante-* means "before": *an antebellum house* (a house built before the [Civil] War); *antedate* (to date before). *Anti-* means "against": *antifeminine, antiseptic*. Hyphenate before capitals, and before *i*: *anti-American, anti-intellectual*.

Anxious. Use to indicate *Angst*, agony, and anxiety. Does not mean cheerful expectation: "He was *anxious* to get started." Use *eager* instead.

Any. Do not overuse as a modifier:

POOR	GOOD
He was the best of any senior in the class.	He was the best senior in the class.
If any people know the answer, they aren't talking.	If anyone knows the answer, he's not talking.

Anybody. Don't write it as two words—*any body*—unless you mean "any corpse," or other inanimate object (stellar body, body of water).

Any more. Always written as two words.

Anyone. Don't write it as two words—*any one*—unless you mean "any one thing."

Anyplace, someplace.   Use *anywhere* and *somewhere* (adverbs), unless you mean "any *place*" and "some *place*."

Appear.   Badly overworked for *seem.*

Appearing.   Don't write "an expensive-appearing house." "An expensive-looking house" is not much better. Write "an expensive house," or "the house looked expensive."

Appreciate.   Means "recognize the worth of." Do not use to mean simply "understand."

LOOSE	CAREFUL
I appreciate your position.	I understand your position.
I appreciate that your position is grotesque.	I realize that your position is grotesque.

Area.   Drop it. *In the area of finance* means *in finance.* Be specific.

POOR	GOOD
This chart is conclusive in all areas.	This chart is conclusive.
	This chart thoroughly displays all departments.

Around.   Do not use for *about:* it will seem to mean "surrounding."

POOR	GOOD
Around thirty people came.	About thirty people came.
He sang at around ten o'clock.	He sang at about ten o'clock.

As.   Use where the cigarette people have *like:* "It tastes good, *as* a goody should." (See also *Like.*)

Do not use for *such as:* "Many things, *as* nails, hats, toothpicks . . . ." Write "Many things, *such as* nails . . . ."

Do not use for *because* or *since;* it is ambiguous:

AMBIGUOUS	PRECISE
As I was walking, I had time to think.	*Since* I was walking, I had time to think.

Do not use *as* to mean "that" or "whether" (as in "I don't know *as* he would like her").

As . . . as.   Use positively, not forgetting the second *as:*

WRONG	RIGHT
as long if not longer than the other.	*as* long *as* the other, if not longer.

Negatively, use *not so . . . as:*

It is *not so* long *as the* other.

His argument is *not so* clear *as* it ought to be.

His argument is *neither so* clear *nor so* thorough *as* it ought to be.

As far as.   A wordy windup.

WORDY	IMPROVED
As far as winter wraps are concerned, she is well supplied.	She has a good supply of winter wraps.

As if.   Takes the subjunctive:

as if he *were* cold

As of, as of now.   Avoid, except for humor. Use *at,* or delete entirely.

POOR	IMPROVED
He left as of ten o'clock.	He left at ten o'clock.
As of now, I've sworn off.	I've sworn off.
	I've just sworn off.

As to.   Use only at the beginning of a sentence: "As to his first allegation, I can only say . . . ." Change it to *about,* or omit it, within a sentence: "He knows nothing *about* the details"; "He is not sure [as to] [whether] they are right."

As well as.   You may mean only *and.* Check it out.

At.   Do not use after *where.* "Where is it *at?*" means "Where is it?"

Back of, in back of.   *Behind* says it more smoothly.

Balance, bulk.   Make them mean business, as in "He deposited the balance of his allowance" and "The bulk of the crop was ruined." Do not use them for people.

POOR	IMPROVED
The balance of the class went home.	The rest of the class went home.
The bulk of the crowd was indifferent.	Most of the crowd was indifferent.

Basis.   Drop it: *on a daily basis* means *daily.*

Behalf—in your behalf, on your behalf.   A nice distinction. "He did it *in your behalf*" means he did it in your interest. "He did it *on your behalf*" means he was representing you, speaking for you.

Besides.   Means "in addition to," not "other than."

POOR	IMPROVED
Something besides smog was the cause [unless smog was also a cause].	Something other than smog was the cause.

Better than. Unless you really mean *better than,* use *more than.*

POOR	IMPROVED
The lake was better than two miles across.	The lake was more than two miles across.

Between, among. *Between* ("by twain") has *two* in mind; *among* has several. *Between,* a preposition, takes an object; *between us, between you and me.* ("Between you and I" is sheer embarrassment; see *me,* below.) But words sometimes fail us. "Between you and me and the gatepost" cannot conform to the rule and become "among you and me and the gatepost." *Between* connotes an intimate sharing *among* all concerned, each to each. *Between* also indicates geographical placing: "It is midway between Chicago, Detroit, and Toledo." "The grenade fell between Jones and me and the gatepost"; but "The grenade fell among the fruit stands." Keep *between* for two and *among* for three or more—unless sense forces a compromise. "Between every building was a plot of petunias" conveys the idea, however nonsensical "between a building" is. "Between all the buildings were plots of petunias" would be better, though still a compromise.

Bimonthly, biweekly. Careless usage has damaged these almost beyond recognition, confusing them with *semimonthly* and *semiweekly.* For clarity, better say "every two months" and "every two weeks."

But, cannot but. "He can but fail" is old but usable. After a negative, however, the natural turn in *but* causes confusion:

POOR	IMPROVED
He cannot *but* fail.	He can only fail.
He could not doubt but that it	He could not doubt that it . . . .
He could not help but take	He could not help taking . . . .

Similarly, *but's* too close or frequent keep your reader spinning:

POOR	IMPROVED
The campaign was successful *but* costly. *But* the victory was sweet.	The campaign was costly, but victory was sweet.

When *but* means "except", it is a preposition.

WRONG	RIGHT
Everybody laughed but I.	Everybody laughed but me.

But that, but what. Colloquial redundancies.

POOR	IMPROVED
There is no doubt but that John's is the best steer.	There is no doubt that John's is the best steer.
	John's is clearly the best steer.
There is no one but what would enjoy it.	Anyone would enjoy it.

Can't hardly, couldn't hardly.   Use *can hardly, could hardly.*

Capability.   Say *it does* or *can do,* not *it has the capability for.*

Case.   Chop out this deadwood:

POOR	IMPROVED
In many cases, ants survive	Ants often . . . .
In such a case, surgery is recommended.	Then surgery is recommended.
In case he goes	If he goes . . . .
Everyone enjoyed himself, except in a few scattered cases.	Almost everyone enjoyed himself.

Cause-and-effect relationship.   Verbal adhesive tape. Recast the sentence, with some verb other than the wordy *cause:*

POOR	IMPROVED
Othello's jealousy rises in a cause-and-effect relationship when he sees the handerchief.	Seeing the handkerchief arouses Othello's jealousy.

Center around.   A physical impossibility. Make it: *centers on,* or *revolves around,* or *concerns,* or *is about.*

Circumstances.   *In these circumstances* makes more sense than *under these circumstances,* since the stances are standing around (*circum*), not standing under.

Clichés.   Don't use unwittingly. But they can be effective. There are two kinds: (1) the rhetorical—*tried and true, the not too distant future, sadder but wiser, in the style to which she had become accustomed;* (2) the proverbial—*apple of his eye, skin of your teeth, sharp as a tack, quick as a flash, twinkling of an eye.* The rhetorical ones are clinched by sound alone; the proverbial are metaphors caught in the popular fancy. Proverbial clichés can lighten a dull passage. You may even revitalize them, since they are frequently dead metaphors (see pp. 84–86). Avoid the rhetorical clichés unless you turn them to your advantage: *tried and untrue, gladder and wiser, a future not too distant.*

Compare to, compare with. To compare *to* is to show similarities (and differences) between different kinds; to compare *with* is to show differences (and similarities) between like kinds.

Composition has been compared *to* architecture.
He compares favorably *with* Mickey Spillane.
Compare Shakespeare *with* Ben Jonson.

Comparisons. Make them complete; add a *than:*

It is more like a jigsaw *than a rational plan.*
They are more thoughtful *than the others.*
The first is better *than the second.* (Or "The first is *the* better.")

Concept. Often jargonish and wordy.

POOR	IMPROVED
The concept of multiprogramming allows	Multiprogramming allows . . . .

Connected with, in connection with. Always wordy. Say *about, with,* or *in.*

POOR	IMPROVED
They discussed several things connected with history.	They discussed several historical questions.
They liked everything in connection with the university.	They liked everything about the university.
He is connected with the Smith Corporation.	He is with the Smith Corporation.

Consider, consider as. The first means "believe to be"; the second, "think about" or "speak about": "I consider him excellent." "I consider him first as a student, then as a man."

Contact. Don't *contact* anyone: get in touch with him, call him, write him, find him, tell him. Don't make a good *contact,* make a helpful friend.

Continual, continuous. You can improve your writing by *continual* practice, but the effort cannot be *continuous.* The first means "frequently repeated"; the second, "without interruption."

It requires continual practice.
There was a continuous line of clouds.

Could care less. You mean *couldn't care less.* Speech has worn off the *n't,* making the words say the opposite of what you mean. A person who cares a great deal could care a great deal less; one who does not care "couldn't care less."

Couple. Use *two, a few,* or *several.* Only the breeziest occasions will allow *a couple of.*

Curriculum. The plural is *curricula,* though *curriculums* will get by; the adjective is *curricular.*

The school offers three separate curricula.
Extracurricular activities also count.

Data. A plural, like *curricula, strata, phenomena:*

The data are inconclusive.

Definitely. A high-school favorite, badly overused.

Different than. Never use it. Things differ *from* each other. Only in comparing differences could *than* be used: "All three of his copies differ from the original, but his last one is *more* different *than* the others." But here *than* is controlled by *more,* not by *different.*

WRONG	RIGHT
It is different *than* I expected.	It is different *from* what I expected.
	It is not what I expected.
This is different *than* all the others.	This is different *from* all the others.

Disinterested. Does not mean "uninterested" nor "indifferent." *Disinterested* means impartial, without private interests in the issue.

WRONG	RIGHT
You seem disinterested in the case.	You seem uninterested in the case.
	The judge was disinterested and perfectly fair.
He was disinterested in it.	He was indifferent to it.

Due to. Never begin a sentence with "*Due* to circumstances beyond his control, he . . . ." *Due* is an adjective and must always relate to a noun or pronoun: "The catastrophe *due to* circumstances beyond his control was unavoidable," or "The catastrophe was *due* to circumstances beyond his control" (predicate adjective). But you are still better off with *because of, through, by,* or *owing to. Due to* is usually a symptom of wordiness, especially when it leads to *due to the fact that.*

WRONG	RIGHT
He resigned due to sickness.	He resigned because of sickness.
He succeeded due to hard work.	He succeeded through hard work.

He lost his shirt due to leaving it in the locker room.	He lost his shirt by leaving it in the locker room.
The Far East will continue to worry the West, due to a general social upheaval.	The Far East will continue to worry the West, owing to a general social upheaval.

Due to the fact that.   A venerable piece of plumbing meaning *because.*

JARGON	IMPROVED
The program failed due to the fact that a recession had set in.	The program failed because a recession had set in.

Effect.   As a noun, it means "result"; as a verb, "to bring about" (not to be confused with *to affect,* meaning "to concern, impress, touch, move"—or "to pretend."

What was the effect?
He effected a thorough change.
How did it affect you?

But note that "He effected a change" is wordy for "He changed."

Enormity.   Means "atrociousness"; does not mean "enormousness."

the enormity of the crime
the enormousness of the mountain

Enthuse.   Don't use it; it coos and gushes:

WRONG	RIGHT
She *enthused* over her new dress.	She gushed on and on about her new dress.
He was *enthused.*	He was enthusiastic.

Environment.   Business jargon, unless you mean the world around us.

WORDY	IMPROVED
in an MVT environment	in MVT; with MVT; under MVT
He works in the environment of cost analysis.	He analyzes costs.
We need to improve the landscaping in the environment of the offices.	We must improve the landscaping around the offices.

Equally as good.   A redundant mixture of two choices, *as good as* and *equally good.* Use only one of these at a time.

Etc.   Substitute something specific for it, or drop it, or use something like "and so forth":

POOR	IMPROVED
She served fruit, cheese, candies, etc.	She served fruit, cheese, candies, and little sweet pickles.

> She served fruit, cheese, candies, and the like.

Ethic. A mannered rendition of *ethics*, the singular and plural noun meaning a system or science of moral principles. Even poorer as an adjective for *ethical*.

Exists. Another symptom of wordiness.

POOR	IMPROVED
a system like that which exists at the university	a system like that at the university

Facet. This means "little face," as on a diamond. Use metaphorically or not at all.

POOR	IMPROVED
This problem has several facets.	This problem has five parts. Each facet of the problem sparkles with implications.

The fact that. Deadly with *due to,* and usually wordy by itself.

POOR	IMPROVED
The fact that Rome fell due to moral decay is clear.	That Rome fell through moral decay is clear.
This disparity is in part a result of the fact that some of the best indicators make their best showings in an expanding market.	This disparity arises in part because some of the best indicators . . . .
In view of the fact that more core is installed	Because it has more core . . . .

Factor. Avoid it. We've used it to death. Try *element* when you mean "element." Look for an accurate verb when you mean "cause."

POOR	IMPROVED
The increase in female employment is a factor in juvenile delinquency.	The increase in female employment has contributed to juvenile delinquency.
Puritan self-sufficiency was an important factor in the rise of capitalism.	Puritan self-sufficiency favored the rise of capitalism.

Farther, further. The first means distance; the second means time or figurative distance. You look *farther* and consider *further*.

The field of. Try to omit it—you usually can—or bring the metaphor to life.

POOR	IMPROVED
He is studying in the field of geology.	He is studying geology.
He changed from the field of science to fine arts.	He moved from the field of science to the green pasture of fine arts.

Firstly.   Archaic. Trim all such terms to *first, second, third,* and so on.

Fix.   The word means "to establish in place"; it means "to repair" only in speech or colloquial writing.

Flaunt, flout.   *Flaunt* means to parade, to wave impudently; *flout* means to scoff at. The first is metaphorical; the second, not: "She *flaunted* her wickedness and *flouted* the police."

Folks.   Use *parents, mother and father,* or *family* instead.

Former, latter.   Passable, but they often make the reader look back. It is better simply to repeat the antecedents.

POOR	IMPROVED
The Athenians and Spartans were always in conflict. *The former* had a better civilization; *the latter* had a better army.	The Athenians and Spartans were always in conflict. Athens had the better culture; Sparta, the better army.

Gray.   America prefers *gray;* England, *grey*—matching our initials.

Hanged, hung.   *Hanged* is the past of *hang* only for the death penalty.
They hung the rope and hanged the man.

Hardly.   Watch the negative here. "I can't *hardly*" means "I *can* easily." Write: "One can hardly conceive the vastness."

Historically.   A favorite windy throat clearer. Badly overused.

Hopefully.   An inaccurate dangler, a cliché. "Hopefully, they are at work" does not mean that they are working hopefully. Simply use "I hope": not "They are a symbol of idealism, and, hopefully, are representative," but "They are a symbol of idealism and are, I hope, representative."

However.   Bury it between commas, or replace it with *but* or *nevertheless.*

POOR	IMPROVED
However, the day had not been entirely lost.	*But* the day had not been entirely lost.
However, the script that Alcuin invented became the forerunner of modern handwriting.	The script that Alcuin invented, *however,* became the forerunner of modern handwriting.

Initial *however* should be an adverb:

However long it takes, it will be done.
However she did it, she did it well.

The idea that.   Like *the fact that*—and the cure is the same.

POOR	IMPROVED
He liked the idea that she was going.	He was pleased she was going.
The idea that space is infinite is difficult to grasp.	That space is infinite is difficult to grasp.

Identify.   Give it an object:

He *identified the wallet.*
He *identified himself* with the hero. (*Not* "He identified with the hero.")

Image.   Resist its popularity, make it mean what it says, and never make it a verb. Do not say, "The university should *image* the handsome intellectual."

Imply, infer.   The author *implies;* you *infer* ("carry in") what you think he means.

He *implied* that all women were hypocrites.
From the ending, we *infer* that tragedy ennobles as it kills.

Importantly.   Often an inaccurate (and popular) adverb, like *hopefully.*

INACCURATE	IMPROVED
More importantly, he walked home.	More important, he walked home.

He did not walk home importantly, nor more importantly.

Includes.   Jargonish, as a general verb for specific actions.

POOR	IMPROVED
The report includes rural and urban marketing.	The report analyzes rural and urban marketing.

Individual.   Write *person,* unless you really mean someone separate and unique.

Inside of, outside of.   "They painted the *outside of* the house" is sound usage; but these expressions can be redundant and inaccurate.

POOR	IMPROVED
inside of half an hour	within half an hour
He had nothing for dinner outside of a few potato chips.	He had nothing for dinner but a few potato chips.

Instances. Redundant. *In many instances* means *often, frequently.*

Interesting. Make what you say interesting, but never tell the reader *it is interesting:* he may not believe you. *It is interesting* is merely a lazy preamble.

POOR	IMPROVED
It is interesting to note that nicotine is named for Jean Nicot, who introduced tobacco into France in 1560.	Nicotine is named for Jean Nicot, who introduced tobacco into France in 1560.

Irony. Not the same as *sarcasm* (which see). A clash between appearance and reality. Irony may be either comic or tragic, depending on your view. But, comic or tragic, irony is of three essential kinds:

Verbal irony. You say the opposite of what you mean: "It's a *great* day," appearing to mean "great" but really meaning "terrible."

Dramatic irony. Someone unwittingly states, or acts upon, a contrariety to the truth. A character in a play, for example, might say "This is my great day," and dance a jig, when the audience has just seen his daughter abducted and the mortgage foreclosed.

Irony of circumstance. The opposite of what ought to happen happens (it rains on the day of the Weather Bureau's picnic; the best man of all is killed); and we are sharply aware of the contrast.

Irregardless. No such word. The *ir-* (meaning *not*) is doing what the *-less* already does. You are thinking of *irrespective,* and trying to say *regardless.*

Is when, is where. Avoid these loose attempts.

LOOSE	SPECIFIC
Combustion is when oxidation bursts into flame.	Combustion is oxidation bursting into flame.
"Trivia" is where three roads meet.	"Trivia" is the place where three roads meet.

-ize. A handy way to make verbs from nouns and adjectives (*patronize, civil-ize*). But handle with care. Manufacture new *-izes* only with a sense of humor and daring ("they Harvardized the party"). Business overdoes the trick: *finalize,* a relative newcomer, has provoked strong disapproval from writers who are not commercially familiarized.

Kind of, sort of. Colloquialisms for *somewhat, rather, something,* and the like. "It is *kind of* odd" will not get by. But "It is a *kind of* academic hippopotamus" will get by nicely, because *a kind of* means *a species of.* Change "a kind of a poor sport" to "a kind of poor sport," and you will seem as knowledgeable as a scientist.

Lay. Don't use *lay* to mean *lie. Lay* means "to put" and needs an object; *lie* means "to recline." Memorize both their present and past tenses, which are frequently confused:

I *lie* down when I can; I *lay* down yesterday; I have *lain* down often. [Intransitive, no object.]

The hen *lays* an egg; she *laid* one yesterday; she has *laid* four this week. [Transitive, *lays* an object.]

Now I *lay* the book on the table; I *laid* it there yesterday; I have *laid* it there many times.

Lend, loan. Don't use *loan* for *lend. Lend* is the verb; *loan,* the noun: "Please *lend* me a five; I need a *loan* badly." Remember the line from the song: "I'll *send* you to a *friend* who'll be willing to *lend.*"

Less, few. Do not use one for the other. *Less* answers "How much?" *Few* answers "How many?"

WRONG	RIGHT
We had *less* people than last time.	We had *fewer* people this time than last.

Like, as, as if. Usage blurs them, but the writer should distinguish them before he decides to go colloquial. Otherwise, he may throw his readers off.

He looks *like* me.
He dresses *as* I do.
He acts *as if* he were high.

Note that *like* takes the objective case, and that *as,* being a conjunction, is followed by the nominative:

She looks like *her.*
He is as tall as *I* [am].
He is tall, like *me.*

The pattern of the prepositional phrase (*like me, like a house, like a river*) has caused *like* to replace *as* where no verb follows in phrases other than comparisons (*as . . . as*):

It works *like* a charm. (. . . *as* a charm *works.*)
It went over *like* a lead balloon. (. . . *as* a lead balloon *does.*)
They worked *like* beavers. (. . . *as* beavers *do.*)

Notice that *as* would give these three statements a meaning of substitution or disguise: "It works as a charm" (but it really isn't a charm); "It went over as a lead balloon" (disguised as a lead balloon).

Manner. Drop this from your working vocabulary. *In a . . . manner* is a favorite redundancy. Replace it with an adverb: *in a clever manner* means "cleverly"; *in an awkward manner* means "awkwardly."

Maximum (minimum) amount. Drop *amount.* The minimum and the maximum *are* amounts. Don't write *a minimum of* and *as a minimum:* write *at least.*

Me. Use *me* boldly. It is the proper object of verbs and prepositions. Nothing is sadder than faulty propriety: "between you and *I*," or "They gave it to John and *I*," or "They invited my wife and *I*." Test yourself by dropping the first member: "between I" (*no*), "gave it to I" (*no*), "invited I" (*no*). And do NOT substitute *myself.*

Medium, media. The singular and the plural. Avoid *medias,* and you will distinguish yourself from the masses.

Most. Does not mean *almost.*

WRONG	RIGHT
Most everyone knows.	Almost everyone knows.

Myself. Use it only reflexively ("I hurt *myself*"), or intensively ("I *myself* often have trouble"). Fear of *me* leads to the incorrect "They gave it to John and *myself*." Do not use *myself, himself, herself, themselves* for *me, him, her, them.*

Nature. Avoid this padding. Do not write *moderate in nature, moderate by nature, of a moderate nature;* simply write *moderate.*

Near. Avoid using it for degree:

POOR	IMPROVED
a near perfect orbit	a nearly perfect orbit
	an almost perfect orbit
We are nowhere near knowledgeable enough.	We are not nearly knowledgeable enough.
It was a near disaster.	It was nearly a disaster [*or* nearly disastrous].

None. This pronoun means "no one" and takes a singular verb, as do *each, every, everyone, nobody,* and other distributives. *None are* has been common and admissible for centuries, but *none is* holds its own, with a certain prestige, even in the daily newspaper. Another pronoun referring back to any of these must also be singular.

POOR	IMPROVED
None of them *are* perfect.	None of them *is* perfect.
Every one of the men *eat* a big breakfast.	Every one of the men *eats* a big breakfast.

| Everybody thinks *they have* the worst of it. | Everybody thinks *he has* the worst of it. |

No one. Two words in America, not *noone,* nor *no-one* (which the British prefer).

Off of. Write *from:* "He jumped *from* his horse."

One. Avoid this common redundancy.

POOR	IMPROVED
One of the most effective ways of writing is rewriting.	The best writing is rewriting.
The Ambassadors is one of the most interesting of James's books.	*The Ambassadors* is James at his best.
The meeting was obviously a poor one.	The meeting was obviously poor.

In constructions such as "one of the best that . . ." and "one of the worst who . . . ," the relative pronouns often are mistakenly considered singular. The plural noun of the prepositional phrase (*the best, worst*), not *the one,* is the antecedent, and the verb must be plural too:

WRONG	RIGHT
one of the best [*players*] who *has* ever swung a bat	one of the best [*players*] who *have* ever swung a bat

Only. Don't put it in too soon; you will say what you do not mean.

WRONG	RIGHT
He *only liked* mystery stories.	He liked *only mystery stories.*

Participle for gerund. Avoid this frequent confusion of the -*ing*'s. The participle works as an adjective; the gerund, as a noun. You want gerunds in the following constructions, and you can get them by changing the misleading noun or pronoun to the possessive case:

WRONG	RIGHT
Washington commended *him passing* through the British lines.	Washington commended *his passing* through the British lines.
Do you mind *me staying* late?	Do you mind *my staying* late?
She disliked *Bill smoking.*	She disliked *Bill's smoking.*
We all enjoyed *them singing* songs and *having* a good time.	We all enjoyed *their singing* songs and *having* a good time.

You can catch these errors by asking yourself if you mean that "Washington commended *him,*" or that "She disliked *Bill*" (which you do not).

Per.   Use *a:* "He worked ten hours *a* day." *Per* is jargonish.

POOR	IMPROVED
This will cost us a manhour per machine per month a year from now.	A year from now, this will cost us a manhour a machine a month.

Perfect.   Not "more perfect," but "more nearly perfect."

Personal.   Change "personal friend" to "good friend," and protect him from seeming too personal.

Personally.   Always superfluous.

POOR	IMPROVED
I want to welcome them *personally.*	I want to welcome them [myself].
Personally, I like it.	I like it.

Phase.   *Phase* is not *faze* ("daunt"), nor does it mean *aspect* or *part;* it is a stage in a familiar cycle, like that of the moon or the caterpillar. Unless you can carry the specific metaphor, avoid it, along with *facet.*

Picket.   A pointed fence post, or a person so staked. *To picket* is to deploy people as pickets, or to join with others as a protesting fence against wrongs.

POOR	IMPROVED
They began a picket of	They began to picket . . . .
They began their picket	They began picketing . . . .
Until they withdraw their picket	Until they withdraw their pickets . . . .

Plan on.   Use *plan to.*

WRONG	RIGHT
He planned on going.	He planned to go.

Power vacuum.   A physical contradiction. Delete the *power,* or put it where it belongs, and your phrase will be accurate.

Provide.   If you *absolutely cannot* use the meaningful verb directly, you may say *provide,* provided you absolutely cannot *give, furnish, allow, supply, enable, authorize, permit, facilitate, force, do, make, effect, help, be, direct, cause, encourage* . . . .

Prejudice.   The illiterate are beginning to write "He was *prejudice.*" Their readers are outrage.

Proof, evidence.   *Proof* results from enough *evidence* to establish a point beyond doubt. Be modest about claiming proof:

POOR	IMPROVED
This *proves* that Fielding was in Bath at the time.	Evidently, Fielding was in Bath at the time.

Proved, proven.   *Proved* is the past participle, which may serve as an adjective meaning "successfully tested or demonstrated"; *proven* is an adjective only, and means "tested by time":

WRONG	RIGHT
It has proven true. [past part.]	It has proved true.
a proven theory [past part. as adj.]	a proved theory
The theory was proven. [same]	The theory was proved.
a proved remedy [pure adj.]	a proven remedy

Quality.   Keep it as a noun. Too many *professional quality writers* are already cluttering our prose, and *poor in quality* means *poor*.

Quote, quotation.   Quote your quotations, and put them in quotation marks. Distinguish the verb from the noun. The best solution is to use *quote* as a verb and to find synonyms for the noun: *passage, remark, assertion.*

WRONG	RIGHT
As the following quote from Milton shows:	As the following passage from Milton shows: . . . .

Real.   Do not use for *very. Real* is an adjective meaning "actual":

WRONG	RIGHT
It was *real* good.	It was *very* good.
	It was *really* good.

Reason . . . is because.   Knock out *the reason . . . is,* and you will have a good sentence.

[The reason] they have difficulty with languages [is] because they have no interest in them.

Regarding, in regard to.   Redundant or inaccurate.

POOR	IMPROVED
Regarding the banknote, Jones was perplexed. [Was he *looking* at it?]	Jones was perplexed by the banknote.
He knew nothing *regarding* money.	He knew nothing about money.
She was careful *in regard to* the facts.	She respected the facts.

Respective, respectively.   Redundant.

POOR	IMPROVED
The armies retreated to their *respective* trenches.	The armies retreated to their trenches.
Smith and Jones won the first and second prize *respectively*.	Smith won the first prize; Jones, the second.

Round. British for *around.*

Sanction. Beatifically ambiguous, now meaning both "to approve" and "to penalize." But why contribute to confusion? Stick to the root; use it only "to bless," "to sanctify," "to approve," "to permit." Use *penalize* or *prohibit* when you mean just that.

POOR	IMPROVED
They exacted sanctions.	They exacted penalties.

Sarcasm. The student's word for irony. Sarcasm intends personal hurt. It may also be ironic, but need not be. "Well, little man, what now?" is pure sarcasm when a dwarf interrupts the class; it is ironic sarcasm when a seven-footer bursts in. See *Irony.*

Shall, will; should, would. The older distinctions—*shall* and *should* reserved for *I* and *we*—have faded; *will* and *would* are usual: "I will go"; "I would if I could"; "he will try"; "they all would." *Shall* in the third person expresses determination: "They shall not pass."

Similar to. Use *like:*

POOR	IMPROVED
This is *similar to* that.	This is *like* that.

Situation. Avoid it. Say what you mean: *state, market, mess, quandary, conflict* . . .

Slow. GO SLOW is what the street signs and the men on the street all say, but write "Go slowly."

So. Should be followed by *that* in describing extent: "It was *so* foggy *that* traffic almost stopped." Avoid its incomplete form, the schoolgirl's intensive—*so nice, so wonderful, so pretty*—though occasionally this is effective.

Split infinitives. Improve them. They are cliché traps: *to really know, to really like, to better understand.* They are misleaders: *to better* . . . , *to further* . . . , *to well* . . . , *to even* . . . , all look and sound like complete infinitives: *to further investigate* starts out like *to further our investigation,* throwing the reader momentarily off the track. *To better know* is to make *know* better, *to even like* is to make *like* even, all of which is nonsense. Indeed, in perverse moments *to eventually* *go* seems to say that *go* is being "eventualied." They are one of the signs of a wordy writer; they are usually redundant: *to really understand* is *to understand.* The quickest cure for split infinitives is to drop the adverb.

Even the splitters do not recommend splitting as a rule. The rule remains DON'T SPLIT; and if you must, learn what you are doing—a little deviltry is better for the soul than ignorance. But I am convinced that you can always mend the split for a gain in grace, and often for a saving of words. You can sometimes change the adverb to an adjective, gaining force; saving letters and words:

POOR	IMPROVED
to adequately think out solutions	to think out adequate solutions
to enable us to effectively plan our advertising	to enable us to plan effective advertising

Or you can drop the adverb—often exuberant—or bring it forward, or move it along:

POOR	IMPROVED
I cannot bring myself to really like the fellow.	I cannot bring myself to like the fellow.
	I cannot bring myself really to like the fellow.
	I really cannot bring myself to like the fellow.

George O. Curme gives the following examples from eminent splitters, arguing that usage makes them right.* But each of them can be improved:

POOR	IMPROVED
I wish the reader to clearly understand this. (Ruskin)	I wish the reader to understand this.
	I wish the reader to understand this clearly.
It would have overburdened the text to there incorporate many details. (Hempl, *Mod. Lang. Notes*)	Details there would have overburdened the text.
. . . without permitting himself to actually mention the name. (Arnold)	. . . without permitting himself to mention the name.
. . . of a kind to directly stimulate curiosity. (Pater)	. . . of a kind to stimulate curiosity.

---

* *English Grammar* (New York: Barnes and Noble, 1947), p. 269.

. . . things which few except
parents can be expected to
really understand. (Oliver
Wendell Holmes)

. . . things only parents can understand.

. . . to bravely disbelieve
(Browning, *The Ring and the
Book*, Cambridge ed., p. 570)

. . . bravely to disbelieve

Browning's full line, in fact, would have thumped somewhat less if
he had dared bravely to vary his meter and mend his infinitive:

Whence need bravely to disbelieve report.

Structure. A darling of the jargoneer, often meaning nothing more
framelike than "unity" or "coherence." *Plot structure* usually means
plot, with little idea of beams and girders. Use it only for something you could diagram, like the ribs of a snake, and never use it
as a verb.

POOR	IMPROVED
He structured the meeting.	He organized (planned, ar-ranged) the meeting.

That, which, who. *That* defines and restricts; *which* is explanatory
and nonrestrictive; *who* stands for people, and may be restrictive or
nonrestrictive. (See pp. 57 and 70.)

The faucet *that* drips is in the basement.

The faucet, *which* drips badly, needs attention.

**Of all the Democrats *who* supported him at first, none was more
ardent than Jones.**

**Of all the Democrats, *who* supported him at first, none was more
ardent than Jones.**

There is, there are, it is. *C'est dangereusement verbeux.* In French,
it is almost as necessary as breathing. In English, it is natural, convenient—AND WORDY. Notice that *it* has here been referring to something specific, differing distinctly from the *it* in "It is easy to write
badly." This indefinite subject, as also do *there is* and *there are,* gives
the trouble. Of course, you will occasionally need an *it* or a *there* to
assert existences:

There are ants in the cupboard.

There is only one Kenneth.

There are craters on the moon.

It is too bad.

But avoid *there is* and *it is,* and you will avoid some sludgy traps.
They are part of the spoken language, like clearing the throat, and

they frequently add just as little, especially when entailing a *that* or a *which:*

There are three men on duty.
[Three men are on duty—5 words for 6.]

There is nothing wrong with this.
[Nothing is wrong with this—5 words for 6.]

There are two things which are important here.
[Two things are important here—5 words for 8.]

It is a habit which few can break.
[Few can break this habit—5 words for 8.]

It is a shame that they had no lawyer.
[Unfortunately, they had no lawyer—5 words for 9.]

They.   A loose indefinite pronoun; tighten it:

POOR	IMPROVED
They are all against us, you know.	*Everyone* is against us, you know.
They launch our rockets at Cape Kennedy.	The *United States* launches its rockets from Cape Kennedy.

Do not use *they* with a singular antecedent.

WRONG	RIGHT
Everyone knows *they* should write correctly.	*Everyone* knows *he* should write correctly.
Every one of the students assumes *they* will pass.	*Every one* of the students assumes *he* will pass.

Till, until.   Both are respectable. Note the spelling. Do not use *'til.*

Too.   Awful as a conjunctive adverb: "Too, it was unjust." Also poor as an intensive: "They did not do too well" (note the difference in Shakespeare's "not wisely but too well"—he really means it). Use *very,* or (better) nothing: "They did not do well" (notice the nice understated irony).

Trite.   From Latin *tritus:* "worn out." Many words get temporarily worn out and unusable: *emasculated, viable, situation,* to name a few. And many phrases are permanently frayed; see *Clichés.*

Try and.   Write *try to. To try and do* means "to try and to do," which is probably not what you mean.

Type.   Banish it, abolish it. If you must use it, insert *of:* not *that type person* but *that type OF person,* though even this is really jargon for *that kind of person, a person like that.* The newspapers have succumbed, and we hear of *commando-type forces* for *commando forces*, of *a Castro-type dictator* for *another Castro*. The most accurate translations of *-type* are *-like, -ish, -esque,* and *-ate,* depending on sense and euphony: *Castro-like, Castro-ish, Russianesque, Italianate.* English has many ways of saying it:

WRONG	RIGHT
essay-type question	essay question
Mondrian's checkerboard-type painting	Mondrian's checkerboard of a painting.
	Mondrian's checkerboardish painting
	Mondrian's checkerboardlike painting
French-type dressing	French dressing
Italian-type spaghetti	Italian spaghetti [Be bold!—we neither know nor care whether it's imported.]
atomic-type submarine	atomic submarine
She was a Brigitte Bardot-type girl.	She was like Brigitte Bardot.
	She was a Brigitte Bardot.
	She was a Brigitte Bardot kind of girl.
	She was a Brigitte Bardot type.
an apprentice-type situation	apprenticeship
a Puck-type person	a Puckish person, a Puck-like person

Unique. Something *unique* has nothing in the world like it.

WRONG	RIGHT
The more unique the organization	The more nearly unique . . . .
the most unique man I know	the most unusual man I know
a very unique personality	a unique personality

Use, use of. A dangerously wordy word. "Through [the use of] personification, he asserts a theme." "In this sense, [the use of] physical detail is significant."

POOR	IMPROVED
He uses personification	He personifies . . . .
He uses inductive reasoning	He reasons inductively . . . .

Utilize, utilization. Wordy. *Utilize* means *use* (verb). *Utilization* means *the use* (noun). And the whole idea of "using"—a basic, universal concept—is frequently contained in the other words of your sentence.

POOR	IMPROVED
He *utilizes* frequent dialogue to enliven his stories.	Frequent dialogue enlivens his stories
The *utilization* of a scapegoat eases their guilt.	A scapegoat eases their guilt.

Very.   Spare the *very* and the *quite, rather, pretty,* and *little.* I would hate to admit (and don't care to know) how many of these qualifiers I have cut from this text. You can do without them entirely.

Ways.   Means *way:* "He went a short *way* into the woods."

While.   Reserve for time only, as in "*While* I was talking, she smoked constantly."

WRONG	RIGHT
While I like her, I don't admire her.	*Although* I like her, I don't admire her.
The side roads were impassable, *while* the highways were clear.	The side roads were impassable, *but* the highways were clear.
The seniors eat in clubs, *while* the freshmen eat in their dormitories.	The seniors eat in clubs, *and* the freshmen eat in their dormitories.

Whom, whomever.   The objective forms, after verbs and prepositions; but each is often wrongly put as the subject of a clause.

WRONG	RIGHT
Give the ticket to *whomever* wants it.	Give the ticket to *whoever wants it.* [The whole clause is the object of *to; whoever* is the subject of *wants.*]
The president, *whom* he said would be late	The president, *who* he said *would be late* . . . . [Commas around *he said* would clear the confusion.]
Whom shall I say called?	*Who* shall I say called?

BUT:

They did not know *whom* to elect. [The infinitive takes the objective case.]

-wise.   Avoid all confections like *marketwise, customerwise, pricewise, gradewise, confectionwise*—except for humor.

Would. For habitual acts, the simple past is more economical:

POOR	IMPROVED
The parliament *would meet* only when called by the king.	The parliament *met* only when called by the king.
Every hour, the watchman *would make* his round.	Every hour, the watchman *made* his round.

Would sometimes seeps into the premise of a supposition. Rule: Don't use *would* in an *if* clause.

WRONG	RIGHT
If he *would have* gone, he would have succeeded.	If he *had* gone, he would have succeeded.
	Had he gone, he would have succeeded [more economical].
I wish I *would have* learned it.	I wish I *had* learned it.

Index

---

* Refer to the Glossary of Usage for troublesome words, prefixes, suffixes, and phrases not listed in the index.